Elevate Your Executive Presence

Your Roadmap to Executive Excellence

Gerard Assey

Elevate Your Executive Presence:
Your Roadmap to Executive Excellence
By
Gerard Assey

Published by:
Gerard Assey
19/18, Palli Arasan Street
Anna Nagar East
Chennai - 600 102

ISBN: 978-81-971121-1-9

Table of Contents

Preface

Part 1: Introduction

- ✓ Understanding Executive Presence
- ✓ The Importance of Executive Presence for Senior Leaders
- ✓ The Missing Link Between Merit and Success
- ✓ Debunking 10 Myths About Executive Presence
- ✓ Benefits of Developing Executive Presence
- ✓ Repercussions of Ignoring Executive Presence
- ✓ Does It Pay to Invest in Executive Presence?
- ✓ Assessing Your Executive Presence and Identifying Areas for Improvement

Part 2: Understanding Executive Presence

- ✓ Characteristics of Executive Presence
- ✓ Traits of Executive Presence- The 10 C's
- ✓ Key Components or Pillars of Executive Presence
- ✓ Mastering Communication for Executive Presence
- ✓ Your Appearance: The Impact of Your Image on Executive Presence
- ✓ Gravitas: The Art of Acting with Executive Presence
- ✓ The Four Categories of Learnable Skills for Executive Presence
- ✓ Character, Substance, Style: The Three Dimensions of Executive Presence

Part 3: Authenticity, Grace, and Poise

- ✓ The Power of Authenticity, Grace, and Poise in Executive Presence
- ✓ The Impact of Authenticity, Grace, and Poise on Leadership Effectiveness
- ✓ Authenticity as Alignment of Head, Mouth, Heart, and Feet

Part 4: Developing Executive Presence

- ✓ Developing Executive Presence
- ✓ A Step-by-Step Action Plan with Checklists for Developing Executive Presence
- ✓ Developing Executive Presence: Exercises and Activities for Practice
- ✓ Tips for Maintaining and Enhancing Executive Presence over Time
- ✓ Identifying Areas for Improvement and Providing/Receiving Feedback
- ✓ Executive Presence in Virtual Settings

Part 5: Commanding Respect like a CEO

- ✓ Commanding Respect like a CEO
- ✓ Displaying Confidence in Meetings
- ✓ Delivering Impactful Presentations
- ✓ Building a Strong Network

Part 6: Maintaining Professionalism: Conclusion

- ✓ Maintaining Professionalism- Positive First Impressions and More
- ✓ Examples of Successful Leaders Exhibiting Executive Presence
- ✓ Conclusion

About the Author

Preface

Welcome to **"Elevate Your Executive Presence: *Your Roadmap to Executive Excellence."*** This book is designed to be your guide on a transformative journey towards mastering the art of executive presence (EP). Whether you are a seasoned leader looking to refine your skills or an aspiring professional aiming to climb the corporate ladder, this book will provide you with the tools, strategies, and insights needed to enhance your EP and achieve your leadership goals.

In today's fast-paced and competitive business world, having executive presence is no longer just a desirable trait; it is a necessity. EP is what sets great leaders apart from the rest, enabling them to command a room, inspire others, and drive results. It is the secret sauce that elevates your leadership effectiveness and propels your career forward.

Through this book, you will learn the key components of EP, including composure, connection, charisma, confidence, credibility, clarity, and conciseness. You will discover how to cultivate authenticity, grace, and poise, and how to leverage these qualities to enhance your leadership impact. Real-life examples and stories of successful leaders will illustrate these concepts, providing you with practical insights that you can apply in your own journey towards EP mastery.

As you embark on this journey, I encourage you to approach it with an open mind and a willingness to challenge yourself. Developing executive presence is not an overnight process; it requires dedication, practice, and a commitment to growth. However, the rewards are immense. By enhancing your EP, you will not only become a more effective leader but also inspire those around you to strive for excellence.

I hope that this book serves as a valuable resource on your path to executive excellence. May it empower you to elevate your presence, unleash your potential, and achieve the success you deserve.

Here's to your journey towards mastering executive presence and becoming the leader you were meant to be.

Part 1:
Introduction

Understanding Executive Presence

In today's fast-paced and competitive business world, being a successful leader requires more than just technical skills and expertise. It requires a certain intangible quality known as executive presence. But what exactly is executive presence, and why is it so crucial for leaders?

Defining Executive Presence

Executive presence is the ability of a leader to project confidence, authority, and authenticity that inspires trust and commands respect. It is the X-factor that sets great leaders apart from the rest. While it is often described as a combination of appearance, communication skills, and demeanor, it is more than just a superficial impression. Executive presence goes beyond what you see on the surface; it is about who you are as a leader and how you show up in the world.

The Components of Executive Presence

- ✓ **Appearance:** While appearance is not the most important aspect of executive presence, it does play a role in how others perceive you. Dressing appropriately for the occasion, grooming oneself well, and paying attention to personal hygiene can all contribute to a positive impression.
- ✓ **Communication Skills:** Effective communication is a key component of executive presence. This includes not just what you say but also how you say it. Clear, concise, and compelling communication can help you connect with others and convey your message effectively.

- ✓ **Demeanor:** Your demeanor, or how you carry yourself, also plays a role in executive presence. This includes your posture, body language, and overall demeanor. A confident, poised demeanor can help you exude authority and inspire confidence in others.

Examples and Stories

To illustrate the concept of executive presence, let's look at a few examples from real life:

- ✓ **Steve Jobs:** The late co-founder and CEO of Apple was known for his charismatic presence and ability to captivate audiences. His passion for innovation and his ability to communicate his vision effectively are prime examples of executive presence.
- ✓ **Sheryl Sandberg:** As the COO of Facebook, Sheryl Sandberg is known for her strong executive presence. She is able to command attention in meetings and has a confident, assertive demeanor that inspires confidence in her leadership.
- ✓ **Nelson Mandela:** The late South African leader Nelson Mandela had a powerful executive presence that helped him lead his country out of apartheid. His grace under pressure and his ability to inspire hope and unity are testament to his strong executive presence.

Executive presence is a critical skill for leaders in today's world. It is about more than just appearance; it is about projecting confidence, authority, and authenticity in everything you do. In the following chapters, we will explore the various components of executive presence in more detail and provide practical tips on how to develop and maintain it.

The Importance of Executive Presence for Senior Leaders

In today's dynamic and competitive business environment, senior leaders face unique challenges that require more than just technical expertise. They must also possess strong leadership qualities, including executive presence. In this chapter, we will explore why executive presence is crucial for senior leaders in today's world.

- ✓ **Establishing Credibility and Influence**
  One of the key reasons why executive presence is important for senior leaders is that it helps establish credibility and influence. When a leader exudes confidence, authority, and authenticity, they are more likely to gain the respect and trust of their team members, peers, and stakeholders. This credibility and influence are essential for senior leaders to effectively lead their teams and drive organizational success.
- ✓ **Inspiring Confidence and Motivation**
  Senior leaders with executive presence have the ability to inspire confidence and motivation in others. Their demeanor, communication skills, and overall presence can have a profound impact on the morale and motivation of their team members. By projecting confidence and positivity, senior leaders can create a supportive and empowering work environment where employees feel motivated to perform at their best.
- ✓ **Navigating Challenges and Uncertainty**

In today's rapidly changing business landscape, senior leaders often face complex challenges and uncertainty. Executive presence can help leaders navigate these challenges with confidence and composure. By projecting a sense of calm and stability, senior leaders can instill confidence in their team members and stakeholders, even in the face of uncertainty.

- ✓ **Driving Organizational Change**
  Senior leaders are often responsible for driving organizational change. Executive presence is crucial in this regard, as it can help leaders communicate the vision for change effectively and inspire others to embrace it. Leaders with strong executive presence are more likely to successfully lead their organizations through periods of change and transformation.

Examples and Stories

To illustrate the importance of executive presence for senior leaders, let's look at a few examples:

- ✓ **Indra Nooyi:** As the former CEO of PepsiCo, Indra Nooyi demonstrated strong executive presence throughout her tenure. She was known for her confident and charismatic leadership style, which helped her drive significant growth and innovation at PepsiCo.
- ✓ **Satya Nadella:** The CEO of Microsoft, Satya Nadella, is another example of a leader with strong executive presence. His ability to communicate Microsoft's vision for the future and inspire his team members has been instrumental in the company's success under his leadership.

- ✓ **Mary Barra:** As the CEO of General Motors, Mary Barra has shown exceptional executive presence in leading the company through challenging times. Her calm and composed demeanor, coupled with her clear communication style, have helped her navigate crises and drive positive change at GM.

In conclusion, executive presence is essential for senior leaders in today's world. It helps establish credibility and influence, inspire confidence and motivation, navigate challenges and uncertainty, and drive organizational change. In the following chapters, we will delve deeper into the characteristics of executive presence and provide practical tips on how senior leaders can develop and enhance this critical skill.

The Missing Link Between Merit and Success

In the corporate world, success is often thought to be directly linked to merit - the idea that hard work, skills, and qualifications are the key determinants of success. However, there is a missing link between merit and success, and that link is executive presence. In this chapter, we will explore how executive presence bridges the gap between merit and success for senior leaders.

Understanding the Gap

While merit is undoubtedly important, it is not always enough to guarantee success. Many talented individuals with impressive credentials struggle to advance in their careers because they lack the executive presence necessary to command respect and influence others. Executive presence is the intangible quality that sets these individuals apart and propels them to success.

The Role of Executive Presence

Executive presence plays a crucial role in helping senior leaders achieve success by enhancing their ability to influence, inspire, and lead effectively. It is the X-factor that enables leaders to make a lasting impact and stand out in a crowded field of talented individuals. Leaders with strong executive presence are able to communicate their vision with clarity and conviction, inspire others to follow their lead, and navigate complex challenges with confidence and composure.

Examples and Stories

Consider the story of Sarah, a highly skilled engineer who struggled to advance in her career despite her

impressive technical skills. Sarah's lack of executive presence made it difficult for her to gain the respect and trust of her colleagues and superiors. However, after working on developing her executive presence, Sarah was able to transform her career and rise to a leadership position within her organization.
Another example is John, a charismatic and confident leader who was able to inspire his team to achieve great success. John's strong executive presence helped him gain the respect and admiration of his team members, enabling him to lead them to new heights of performance and success.

In conclusion, executive presence is the missing link between merit and success for senior leaders. By developing this crucial skill, leaders can enhance their ability to influence, inspire, and lead effectively, ultimately propelling them to greater success in their careers. In the following chapters, we will explore practical strategies for developing and enhancing executive presence for senior leaders.

Debunking 10 Myths About Executive Presence

Executive presence is often surrounded by myths and misconceptions that can hinder leaders from developing this critical skill. In this chapter, we will debunk 10 common myths about executive presence and provide clarity on what it truly entails.

- ✓ **Myth 1: Executive Presence is All About Appearance**
  While appearance is a component of executive presence, it is not the only factor. Executive presence is also about how you communicate, behave, and lead.
- ✓ **Myth 2: Executive Presence is Inborn and Cannot be Developed**
  Contrary to popular belief, executive presence is a skill that can be developed and honed over time with practice and effort.
- ✓ **Myth 3: Executive Presence is Only Important for Senior Leaders**
  Executive presence is important at all levels of an organization, as it contributes to effective communication, leadership, and influence.
- ✓ **Myth 4: Executive Presence is the Same as Charisma**
  While charisma can be a part of executive presence, it is not the defining factor. Executive presence is more about how you conduct yourself and communicate with others.
- ✓ **Myth 5: Executive Presence Requires Being Extroverted**

Executive presence is not about being extroverted or outgoing. It is about being able to communicate and lead effectively, regardless of your personality type.

- ✓ **Myth 6: Executive Presence is About Being Perfect**
  Executive presence is not about being flawless. It is about being authentic and genuine in your interactions with others.
- ✓ **Myth 7: Executive Presence is About Dominating Conversations**
  Executive presence is actually about being a good listener and communicating effectively, rather than dominating conversations.
- ✓ **Myth 8: Executive Presence is About Being Aggressive**
  Executive presence is not about being aggressive or assertive. It is about being confident and composed in your interactions with others.
- ✓ **Myth 9: Executive Presence is About Having a Loud Voice**
  Executive presence is about having a strong, confident voice, but it is not necessarily about being loud. It is more about how you use your voice to convey your message effectively.
- ✓ **Myth 10: Executive Presence is About Putting on a Persona**
  Executive presence is about being authentic and true to yourself. It is not about putting on a persona or trying to be someone you're not.

Examples and Stories

Consider the story of Alex, a leader who believed that executive presence was all about appearance.

However, after attending a workshop on executive presence, Alex realized that it was about much more than that. By focusing on developing his communication skills and leadership presence, Alex was able to significantly improve his executive presence and advance in his career.
Another example is Sarah, who believed that executive presence required her to be extroverted and dominant in conversations. However, after receiving feedback from her colleagues, Sarah learned that executive presence was more about being a good listener and communicating effectively. By adjusting her approach, Sarah was able to enhance her executive presence and become a more effective leader.

In conclusion, executive presence is often misunderstood, leading to myths and misconceptions. By debunking these myths and gaining a clearer understanding of what executive presence truly entails, leaders can take the necessary steps to develop and enhance this critical skill. In the following chapters, we will explore practical strategies for developing executive presence and debunking these myths.

Benefits of Developing Executive Presence

Executive presence (EP) is a valuable asset for both individuals and organizations. In this chapter, we will explore the numerous benefits of developing executive presence, highlighting how it can positively impact both personal and organizational success.

1. **Enhanced Influence and Persuasion**
   Individuals with strong executive presence are more effective at influencing and persuading others. Their ability to communicate clearly and confidently allows them to convey their ideas and proposals convincingly.
2. **Improved Leadership Effectiveness**
   Leaders with executive presence are better able to inspire and motivate their teams. Their confident and composed demeanor instills trust and confidence in their leadership, leading to improved team performance.
3. **Increased Career Opportunities**
   Developing executive presence can open up new career opportunities. Individuals with strong executive presence are often considered for leadership roles and are more likely to be selected for high-profile projects and assignments.
4. **Greater Confidence and Self-Assurance**
   Developing executive presence can boost confidence and self-assurance. Individuals who project confidence and poise are more likely to feel confident in their abilities and decisions.
5. **Enhanced Communication Skills**

Executive presence requires strong communication skills. By developing executive presence, individuals can improve their ability to communicate effectively, both verbally and non-verbally.

6. **Improved Relationship Building**
   Executive presence is also about building strong relationships. Individuals with strong executive presence are better able to connect with others and build rapport, leading to more productive and fulfilling relationships.
7. **Increased Executive Visibility**
   Developing executive presence can increase visibility within an organization. Leaders with strong executive presence are more likely to be noticed and recognized for their contributions.
8. **Enhanced Decision-Making Skills**
   Executive presence requires composure and clarity of thought, which can lead to improved decision-making skills. Individuals with strong executive presence are better able to make sound decisions under pressure.
9. **Better Crisis Management Abilities**
   Leaders with executive presence are often better equipped to handle crises. Their calm and composed demeanor can help them navigate challenging situations effectively.
10. **Positive Organizational Impact**
    Organizations benefit from having leaders with executive presence. Leaders who project confidence and authority can inspire trust and confidence in their teams, leading to a more positive and productive work environment.

Examples and Stories

Consider the story of James, a mid-level manager who decided to focus on developing his executive presence. As a result, James was able to enhance his leadership skills and communication abilities, leading to a promotion to a senior leadership role.

Another example is Sarah, a senior executive who worked on improving her executive presence. Sarah's enhanced presence helped her gain the respect and trust of her colleagues and superiors, leading to increased career opportunities and greater influence within her organization.

In conclusion, developing executive presence offers numerous benefits for both individuals and organizations. From enhanced influence and persuasion to improved leadership effectiveness and career opportunities, the benefits of developing executive presence are vast. In the following chapters, we will explore practical strategies for developing and enhancing executive presence.

Repercussions of Ignoring Executive Presence

While developing executive presence can lead to numerous benefits, ignoring this crucial aspect of leadership can have significant repercussions. In this chapter, we will explore the repercussions of ignoring executive presence, highlighting the negative impact it can have on individuals and organizations.

1. **Limited Career Advancement Opportunities**
   One of the primary repercussions of ignoring executive presence is limited career advancement opportunities. Individuals who lack executive presence may find it challenging to move into leadership roles or secure promotions.
2. **Reduced Influence and Impact**
   Leaders who lack executive presence may struggle to influence and inspire others. Their lack of confidence and composure can diminish their ability to make a meaningful impact within their organizations.
3. **Poor Communication and Relationship Building**
   Executive presence is closely linked to effective communication and relationship building. Leaders who ignore executive presence may struggle to communicate clearly and build strong relationships with their colleagues and teams.
4. **Decreased Confidence and Self-Esteem**
   Ignoring executive presence can also lead to decreased confidence and self-esteem.

Leaders who lack executive presence may doubt their abilities and struggle to assert themselves in professional settings.

5. **Missed Leadership Opportunities**
   Leaders who ignore executive presence may miss out on important leadership opportunities. They may be overlooked for key projects or assignments due to their perceived lack of leadership presence.
6. **Negative Perception by Others**
   Leaders who lack executive presence may be perceived negatively by their colleagues and superiors. They may be seen as lacking in confidence, authority, or credibility, which can hinder their professional growth.
7. **Ineffective Decision-Making**
   Executive presence is associated with composure and clarity of thought, which are essential for effective decision-making. Leaders who ignore executive presence may struggle to make sound decisions under pressure.
8. **Poor Team Morale and Engagement**
   Leaders who lack executive presence may struggle to motivate and engage their teams. Their lack of confidence and clarity can lead to poor team morale and decreased productivity.
9. **Increased Stress and Burnout**
   Leaders who ignore executive presence may experience increased stress and burnout. The pressure to perform without the necessary presence and composure can take a toll on their mental and emotional well-being.
10. **Negative Organizational Impact**

Finally, ignoring executive presence can have a negative impact on the organization as a whole. Leaders who lack executive presence may fail to inspire trust and confidence in their teams, leading to decreased overall performance and morale.

Examples and Stories

Consider the story of Mark, a leader who ignored executive presence and focused solely on technical skills. Despite his impressive qualifications, Mark struggled to advance in his career due to his lack of leadership presence. It was only after he invested in developing his executive presence that he was able to secure a leadership role within his organization.

Another example is Emily, a senior executive who dismissed the importance of executive presence. Emily's lack of presence and composure led to strained relationships with her team members and colleagues, ultimately impacting her ability to lead effectively.

In conclusion, ignoring executive presence can have far-reaching repercussions for individuals and organizations. From limited career advancement opportunities to decreased confidence and impact, the negative effects of ignoring executive presence are significant. In the following chapters, we will explore practical strategies for developing and enhancing executive presence to avoid these repercussions.

Does It Pay to Invest in Executive Presence?

Investing time, energy, and resources in developing executive presence (EP) can be a significant commitment. In this chapter, we will explore whether this investment is worthwhile by examining the returns and benefits of developing executive presence for both individuals and organizations.

- ✓ **Individual Perspective**
  From an individual perspective, investing in executive presence can pay off in several ways. For example, individuals who develop strong executive presence are more likely to be considered for leadership roles and promotions. They are also better equipped to influence and inspire others, leading to increased career opportunities and advancement.
  Consider the story of Alex, a mid-level manager who decided to invest in developing his executive presence. As a result, Alex was able to enhance his leadership skills and communication abilities, leading to a promotion to a senior leadership role.
- ✓ **Organizational Perspective**
  From an organizational perspective, investing in executive presence can also yield significant benefits. Leaders with strong executive presence are better able to inspire and motivate their teams, leading to increased productivity and performance. They are also more effective at driving organizational change and navigating challenges, which can

lead to improved overall organizational success.

For example, Sarah, a senior executive who worked on improving her executive presence, was able to gain the respect and trust of her colleagues and superiors. This increased her influence within the organization and contributed to positive organizational outcomes.

In conclusion, investing in executive presence can pay off both for individuals and organizations. From increased career opportunities and advancement to improved leadership effectiveness and organizational success, the benefits of developing executive presence are significant. In the following chapters, we will explore practical strategies for developing and enhancing executive presence to maximize these returns.

Assessing Your Executive Presence and Identifying Areas for Improvement

Assessing your current level of executive presence (EP) is the first step towards developing and enhancing this critical leadership skill. In this chapter, we will explore how you can assess your executive presence and identify areas for improvement, using a detailed template for self-assessment.

Understanding Executive Presence

Before assessing your executive presence, it is important to understand what it entails. Executive presence is the ability to project confidence, authority, and credibility in your interactions with others. It involves a combination of factors, including communication skills, demeanor, and appearance.

Self-Assessment Template

Communication Skills:

- ✓ How effectively do you communicate your ideas and vision to others?
- ✓ Do you actively listen to others and engage in meaningful dialogue?
- ✓ Rate your ability to speak confidently and persuasively in various settings (e.g., meetings, presentations).

Demeanor:

- ✓ How do you typically conduct yourself in professional settings?
- ✓ Rate your level of composure and confidence in challenging situations.

- ✓ How well do you connect with others and build rapport?

Appearance:

- ✓ How do you present yourself physically (e.g., grooming, attire)?
- ✓ Rate your ability to create a positive first impression through your appearance.
- ✓ How does your appearance align with your professional goals and the expectations of your role?

Leadership Presence:

- ✓ How do others perceive your leadership presence?
- ✓ Rate your ability to inspire and motivate others.
- ✓ How well do you demonstrate authority and credibility in your leadership role?

Feedback:

- ✓ Have you received feedback from others regarding your executive presence?
- ✓ If so, what were the key points of feedback?
- ✓ How have you incorporated this feedback into your development?

Identifying Areas for Improvement

After completing the self-assessment, review your responses to identify areas where you can improve your executive presence. For example, if you rated your communication skills as average, you may want to focus on enhancing your ability to speak confidently and persuasively. Similarly, if you rated your demeanor as lacking composure, you may want to work on managing stress and projecting a more confident demeanor.

Real-Life Example

Consider the story of Rachel, a senior manager who assessed her executive presence and identified a need to improve her communication skills. She enrolled in public speaking courses and practiced delivering presentations to enhance her ability to speak confidently and persuasively. As a result, Rachel saw a significant improvement in how she was perceived by her colleagues and superiors, leading to increased opportunities for advancement.

Executive Presence Self-Assessment Template

Instructions: For each statement, rate yourself on a scale of 1 to 5, with 1 being strongly disagree and 5 being strongly agree. Be honest and reflective in your responses to get an accurate assessment of your executive presence.

Communication Skills

I communicate my ideas and vision clearly and effectively.

1 2 3 4 5

I actively listen to others and engage in meaningful dialogue.

1 2 3 4 5

I speak confidently and persuasively in various settings.

1 2 3 4 5

Demeanor

I conduct myself professionally in all situations.

1 2 3 4 5

I remain composed and confident in challenging situations.

1 2 3 4 5

I connect with others and build rapport easily.

1 2 3 4 5

Appearance

I present myself professionally through grooming and attire.

1 2 3 4 5

I create a positive first impression through my appearance.

1 2 3 4 5

My appearance aligns with my professional goals and role expectations.

1 2 3 4 5

Leadership Presence

Others perceive me as a confident and credible leader.

1 2 3 4 5

I inspire and motivate others to achieve goals.

1 2 3 4 5

I demonstrate authority and credibility in my leadership role.

1 2 3 4 5

Feedback

I have received feedback on my executive presence.

1 2 3 4 5

I have incorporated feedback into my development.

1 2 3 4 5

I actively seek feedback to improve my executive presence.

1 2 3 4 5

Scoring:

Add up your scores for each category (Communication Skills, Demeanor, Appearance, Leadership Presence, Feedback).

- ✓ A score of 25-35 indicates a strong executive presence.

- ✓ A score of 15-24 indicates areas for improvement in executive presence.
- ✓ A score below 15 suggests significant development opportunities in executive presence.

Reflection: After completing the self-assessment, reflect on your scores and identify specific areas where you can improve your executive presence. Consider seeking feedback from colleagues or mentors to gain additional insights and develop a plan for enhancing your executive presence.

Assessing your executive presence is a valuable exercise that can help you identify areas for improvement and develop a plan for enhancing this critical leadership skill. By using this self-assessment template, you can gain valuable insights into your executive presence and take concrete steps towards improving it.

Reflection Questions

- ✓ What does executive presence mean to you, and why is it important in your professional life?
- ✓ Reflect on a situation where you felt you lacked executive presence. What could you have done differently?
- ✓ How do you think enhancing your executive presence could benefit your career and leadership journey?
- ✓ What are some common misconceptions about executive presence that you've encountered, and how do you plan to address them?

- ✓ After assessing your current level of executive presence, what areas do you feel you need to improve, and what steps will you take to do so?

Part 2:
Understanding Executive Presence

Characteristics of Executive Presence

Executive presence (EP) is a multifaceted quality that encompasses a range of characteristics and behaviors. In this chapter, we will explore the key characteristics of executive presence and how they contribute to effective leadership.

1. **Confidence**
   Confidence is a fundamental characteristic of executive presence. Leaders with EP project a sense of self-assurance and belief in their abilities, inspiring confidence in others.
   Consider the story of John, a senior executive who exuded confidence in his leadership role. His confident demeanor helped him navigate challenging situations and inspire his team to achieve their goals.
2. **Composure**
   Composure is another important aspect of executive presence. Leaders with EP remain calm and collected under pressure, demonstrating poise and control in challenging situations.
   For example, Sarah, a CEO, maintained her composure during a crisis, reassuring her team and stakeholders with her calm and decisive leadership.
3. **Charisma**
   Charisma is the ability to attract and charm others. Leaders with EP possess a certain magnetic quality that draws people to them, making them effective communicators and influencers.

Mark, a charismatic leader, had a natural ability to connect with others and inspire them to follow his vision, earning him respect and admiration from his team.

4. **Communication Skills**

   Effective communication is essential for executive presence. Leaders with EP are able to articulate their ideas clearly and persuasively, conveying confidence and credibility.

   Rachel, a senior manager, honed her communication skills to enhance her executive presence, becoming a more influential and impactful leader as a result.

5. **Authenticity**

   Authenticity is about being genuine and true to oneself. Leaders with EP are authentic in their interactions, earning trust and respect from others.

   David, a leader known for his authenticity, was able to build strong relationships with his team members, fostering a culture of trust and collaboration.

6. **Gravitas**

   Gravitas is a sense of seriousness and importance. Leaders with EP command respect and authority, projecting a sense of gravitas that inspires confidence in their leadership.

   Lisa, a senior executive, had a commanding presence that conveyed gravitas, earning her the respect and trust of her colleagues and superiors.

Executive presence is a combination of confidence, composure, charisma, communication skills, authenticity, and gravitas. Leaders who possess these characteristics are able to inspire and influence others, driving organizational success. In the following chapters, we will explore practical strategies for developing these characteristics to enhance your executive presence.

Traits of Executive Presence
The 10 C's

Executive presence (EP) is often characterized by a set of traits that are essential for effective leadership. In this chapter, we will explore the 10 C's of executive presence, including composure, connection, charisma, confidence, credibility, clarity, conciseness, and three additional traits relevant to this subject.

1. **Composure**
   Composure refers to the ability to remain calm and composed under pressure. Leaders with composure are able to think clearly and make sound decisions, even in challenging situations.
   Consider the story of Emily, a CEO who maintained her composure during a crisis, reassuring her team and stakeholders with her calm and decisive leadership.
2. **Connection**
   Connection is about building meaningful relationships with others. Leaders who are able to connect with their team members and colleagues are more effective at inspiring and motivating them.
   John, a leader known for his ability to connect with others, was able to build a strong and loyal team that supported him in achieving his goals.
3. **Charisma**
   Charisma is a quality that attracts and inspires others. Leaders with charisma have a

magnetic personality that draws people to them, making them effective influencers.

Sarah, a charismatic leader, was able to inspire her team to achieve great results through her infectious enthusiasm and passion.

4. **Confidence**

   Confidence is a key trait of executive presence. Leaders who project confidence are more likely to inspire trust and respect in their team members and colleagues.

   David, a confident leader, was able to lead his team with conviction, earning their trust and admiration.

5. **Credibility**

   Credibility is about being trustworthy and reliable. Leaders who are credible are able to earn the trust and respect of their team members and stakeholders.

   Lisa, a leader known for her credibility, was able to build strong relationships with her team members based on trust and respect.

6. **Clarity**

   Clarity is the ability to communicate clearly and effectively. Leaders who are able to communicate their ideas clearly are more likely to be understood and followed by their team members.

   Rachel, a leader known for her clarity of communication, was able to articulate her vision and goals in a way that inspired her team to action.

7. **Conciseness**

   Conciseness is about being clear and to the point in communication. Leaders who are concise are able to convey their message effectively without unnecessary complexity.

Mark, a leader known for his concise communication style, was able to communicate complex ideas in a way that was easy for his team to understand.

8. **Consistency**

   Consistency is the ability to maintain a certain standard or behavior over time. Leaders who are consistent in their actions and decisions are more likely to earn the trust and respect of their team members.

   Emily, a leader known for her consistency, was able to lead her team with a sense of stability and predictability, earning their trust and loyalty.

9. **Creativity**

   Creativity is the ability to think outside the box and come up with innovative solutions. Leaders who are creative are able to inspire their team members to think creatively and solve problems in new ways.

   John, a leader known for his creativity, was able to lead his team to success by encouraging them to think differently and explore new ideas.

10. **Care**

    Care refers to the ability to show empathy and concern for others. Leaders who care about their team members are able to build strong and supportive relationships that foster loyalty and commitment.

    Sarah, a leader known for her care for her team members, was able to create a positive and nurturing work environment where her team members felt valued and supported.

The 10 C's of executive presence - composure, connection, charisma, confidence, credibility, clarity, conciseness, consistency, creativity, and care - are essential traits for effective leadership. Leaders who possess these traits are able to inspire and influence others, driving organizational success. In the following chapters, we will explore practical strategies for developing these traits to enhance your executive presence.

Key Components or Pillars of Executive Presence

Executive presence (EP) is built on a foundation of key components or pillars that encompass various aspects of an individual's professional demeanor. In this chapter, we will explore the three primary components of executive presence: communication skills, appearance, and gravitas, and how they contribute to a leader's overall presence and impact.

1. **Communication Skills**
   Effective communication is at the core of executive presence. Leaders with strong communication skills are able to convey their ideas clearly, influence others, and build strong relationships.
   Consider the example of Michael, a CEO known for his exceptional communication skills. Michael's ability to articulate his vision and engage with his team members effectively contributed to his strong executive presence and leadership effectiveness.
2. **Appearance**
   Appearance plays a significant role in executive presence. How a leader presents themselves physically can greatly impact how they are perceived by others.
   For instance, Jessica, a senior executive, always ensured she was well-groomed and dressed professionally. Her attention to her appearance not only reflected her professionalism but also contributed to her credibility and authority as a leader.
3. **Gravitas**

Gravitas refers to the presence, confidence, and dignity that a leader exudes. It is the intangible quality that commands respect and attention.

John, a senior executive, had a strong sense of gravitas that was evident in his demeanor and interactions with others. His calm and authoritative presence made him a natural leader whom others looked up to and respected.

The key components or pillars of executive presence—communication skills, appearance, and gravitas—are essential for leaders looking to enhance their presence and influence. By focusing on developing these components, leaders can strengthen their executive presence and become more effective in their roles. In the following chapters, we will delve deeper into strategies for improving these key components of executive presence.

Mastering Communication for Executive Presence

Communication is a fundamental aspect of executive presence, encompassing various elements such as listening, questioning, voice tone, eye contact, gestures, and phrasing. In this chapter, we will explore these elements in detail and how they contribute to your overall communication effectiveness as a leader.

1. **Listening Skills**
   Effective listening is crucial for building rapport and understanding the needs and concerns of others. It involves giving your full attention to the speaker, empathizing with their perspective, and providing appropriate responses.
   Example: Sarah, a leader known for her excellent listening skills, always made sure to listen actively to her team members. She would maintain eye contact, nod in agreement, and ask clarifying questions to demonstrate her understanding.
2. **Questioning Techniques**
   Asking thoughtful and probing questions can help you gather information, uncover insights, and engage others in meaningful dialogue. It's important to ask open-ended questions that encourage discussion and exploration.
   Example: John, a CEO, was skilled at asking insightful questions during meetings to stimulate discussion and challenge his team's thinking. His questions often led to innovative solutions and new perspectives.

3. **Voice Tone**
   Your tone of voice can convey a range of emotions and attitudes, influencing how your message is received. It's important to speak clearly and confidently, with a tone that matches the context and content of your message.
   Example: Rachel, a leader with a strong executive presence, had a commanding voice tone that captivated her audience during presentations. Her authoritative tone helped her convey confidence and credibility.
4. **Eye Contact**
   Maintaining eye contact is a powerful way to establish connection and convey sincerity. It shows that you are engaged and attentive, which is essential for building trust and rapport.
   Example: David, a senior executive, made sure to maintain eye contact with his team members during meetings. His eye contact conveyed his interest and respect for their opinions, fostering a sense of inclusion and respect.
5. **Gestures and Body Language**
   Nonverbal cues such as gestures and body language can enhance your message and convey confidence and authority. It's important to use gestures that are natural and expressive, without being overly dramatic.
   Example: Emily, a leader known for her charismatic presence, used gestures and body language to emphasize key points during presentations. Her gestures were purposeful and helped her connect with her audience.

6. **Phrasing and Clarity**
   The way you phrase your words can impact how your message is perceived. It's important to use clear and concise language, avoiding jargon or complex terminology that may confuse or alienate your audience.
   Example: Mark, a leader known for his clear communication style, always made sure to use simple and straightforward language in his emails and presentations. His clarity helped him convey his message effectively and avoid misunderstandings.

Effective communication is a key component of executive presence, encompassing various elements such as listening, questioning, voice tone, eye contact, gestures, and phrasing. By mastering these elements, you can enhance your communication effectiveness and strengthen your executive presence as a leader. In the following chapters, we will explore practical strategies for improving your communication skills to enhance your executive presence.

Your Appearance: The Impact of Your Image on Executive Presence

Your appearance plays a crucial role in how you are perceived as a leader. In this chapter, we will explore the importance of appearance in executive presence, including its impact on your credibility, professionalism, and leadership effectiveness. We will also provide grooming tips, discuss the importance of weight and energy management, and offer advice on dressing for success.

1. **Importance and Impact of Appearance**
   Your appearance is often the first impression others have of you, and it can significantly influence how you are perceived in the workplace. A well-groomed and professionally dressed appearance can enhance your credibility and authority as a leader.
   Example: Sarah, a senior executive, always made sure to dress professionally and groom herself impeccably. Her polished appearance not only earned her respect from her colleagues but also helped her establish a strong executive presence.
2. **Grooming Tips**
   Proper grooming is essential for maintaining a professional appearance. This includes regular haircuts, grooming facial hair, and keeping nails clean and trimmed. It's also important to maintain good personal hygiene, such as showering daily and using deodorant.
   Example: John, a CEO, paid attention to his grooming by always keeping his hair neatly trimmed and his facial hair well-groomed. His

attention to detail in his grooming routine contributed to his overall professional image.

3. **Weight and Energy Management**
   Maintaining a healthy weight and high energy levels can also impact your appearance and executive presence. Regular exercise and a balanced diet can help you stay in shape and maintain high energy levels, which are important for projecting vitality and confidence.
   Example: Rachel, a leader, made it a priority to stay fit and healthy by exercising regularly and eating a balanced diet. Her commitment to her health not only improved her appearance but also gave her the energy she needed to lead effectively.
4. **Dressing for Success**
   Your choice of clothing can have a significant impact on how you are perceived in the workplace. Dressing appropriately for your role and the occasion can help you project professionalism and authority.
   Example: David, a senior executive, always dressed in tailored suits and polished shoes. His attention to his attire not only made him look professional but also helped him command respect as a leader.

Your appearance plays a crucial role in your executive presence, influencing how you are perceived as a leader. By paying attention to grooming, weight and energy management, and dressing appropriately, you can enhance your appearance and strengthen your executive presence. In the following chapters, we will explore practical strategies for improving your appearance to enhance your executive presence.

Executive Presence Grooming and Attire Checklist

This checklist is designed to help you ensure your grooming and attire are on point to enhance your executive presence. It covers aspects from head to toe and is suitable for both men and women.

Hair:

☐ Hair is clean, well-groomed, and styled appropriately for the workplace.

☐ If applicable, facial hair is neatly trimmed and well-maintained.

Face:

☐ Skin is clean and well-moisturized.

☐ If applicable, eyebrows are groomed and tidy.

Eyes:

☐ Eyes are clear and alert.

☐ Glasses are clean and in good condition (if worn).

Teeth:

☐ Teeth are clean and well-maintained.

☐ Breath is fresh (use mints or mouthwash if necessary).

Body:

☐ Body odor is not present (use deodorant or antiperspirant if necessary).

☐ Nails are clean and trimmed (including toenails if visible).

Attire:

☐ Clothing is clean, pressed, and free of wrinkles.

☐ Clothing fits well and is appropriate for the workplace (not too tight or too loose).

☐ Colors are coordinated and suitable for your skin tone.

☐ Shoes are clean, polished, and in good condition.

Accessories:

☐ Jewelry is tasteful and not overly flashy.

☐ Watches or other accessories are clean and in good condition.

☐ Belts match shoes in color and are in good condition.

Overall Appearance:

☐ Posture is upright and confident.

☐ Facial expressions are friendly and approachable.

☐ Overall demeanor is professional and polished.

Additional Tips:

☐ Consider the industry and workplace culture when selecting your attire.

☐ Avoid strong perfumes or colognes that may be overpowering.

☐ Regularly review and update your grooming and attire based on feedback and changes in fashion trends.

By using this checklist regularly, you can ensure that your grooming and attire are always on point, helping you enhance your executive presence and make a positive impression in the workplace.

Gravitas: The Art of Acting with Executive Presence

Gravitas is a key component of executive presence, often described as the quality of authority, dignity, and seriousness that a leader exudes. In this chapter, we will explore gravitas in detail, examining the ingredients that make it up and how it can be developed to enhance your executive presence.

1. **Composure**
   Composure is a critical aspect of gravitas, referring to the ability to remain calm and collected in challenging situations. Leaders with composure are able to think clearly and make rational decisions, even under pressure.
   Example: Sarah, a CEO, demonstrated composure when faced with a crisis in her organization. Instead of panicking, she remained calm and focused, reassuring her team and stakeholders with her composed demeanor.
2. **Confidence**
   Confidence is another essential ingredient of gravitas. Leaders who are confident in themselves and their abilities are more likely to inspire trust and respect in others.
   Example: John, a senior executive, exuded confidence in his leadership by speaking with conviction and authority. His confident demeanor inspired confidence in his team and helped him gain the respect of his peers.
3. **Connection**
   Connection refers to the ability to build meaningful relationships with others. Leaders

who are able to connect with their team members and colleagues on a personal level are more likely to be seen as authentic and trustworthy.

Example: Rachel, a leader known for her strong connection with her team, took the time to listen to their concerns and show empathy towards their challenges. Her ability to connect with her team members on a personal level earned her their loyalty and respect.

4. **Clarity**

   Clarity of thought and communication is also essential for gravitas. Leaders who are able to articulate their ideas clearly and concisely are more likely to be understood and respected by others.

   Example: David, a leader known for his clarity of communication, was able to convey complex ideas in a way that was easy for his team to understand. His clear and concise communication style earned him the respect of his team members.

5. **Commitment**

   Commitment to one's values and goals is a hallmark of gravitas. Leaders who are committed to their vision and principles are more likely to inspire others to follow them.

   Example: Emily, a leader known for her unwavering commitment to her values, always acted in alignment with her principles. Her commitment to her values earned her the respect and admiration of her team.

Gravitas is a key component of executive presence, encompassing qualities such as composure, confidence, connection, clarity, and commitment. By developing these qualities, you can enhance your gravitas and become a more effective leader in your organization. In the following chapters, we will explore practical strategies for developing gravitas to enhance your executive presence.

The Four Categories of Learnable Skills for Executive Presence

Executive presence (EP) is not just about innate qualities; it can also be developed through learnable skills. In this chapter, we will explore the four categories of learnable skills that contribute to executive presence: assumptions, actions, communication, and appearance.

1. **Assumptions**
   Assumptions are the beliefs and attitudes that shape how we perceive ourselves and others. Developing positive assumptions about oneself and others is crucial for building executive presence.
   For example, Sarah, a leader, used to doubt her abilities and often assumed that others did not value her opinions. Through coaching and self-reflection, she learned to challenge these assumptions and develop a more positive and confident mindset, which significantly improved her executive presence.
2. **Actions**
   Actions refer to the behaviors and habits that influence how others perceive us. Leaders can enhance their executive presence by adopting actions that reflect their values and priorities.
   Consider the case of Alex, a manager who wanted to improve his executive presence. He started taking on more leadership responsibilities, such as leading team meetings and presenting to senior management, which helped him demonstrate

his capabilities and increase his visibility within the organization.

3. **Communication**
   Communication skills are essential for effective leadership and executive presence. Leaders who can communicate clearly, confidently, and persuasively are more likely to command respect and influence others.
   Rachel, a leader known for her strong executive presence, worked on improving her communication skills by attending public speaking courses and seeking feedback from colleagues. These efforts helped her become a more effective communicator and enhance her executive presence.
4. **Appearance**
   Appearance plays a significant role in how we are perceived by others. Leaders who pay attention to their grooming, attire, and overall presentation are more likely to be seen as professional and credible.
   John, a senior executive, always made sure to dress appropriately for the occasion and maintain a neat and polished appearance. His attention to detail in his appearance contributed to his executive presence and helped him make a positive impression on others.

Developing executive presence is not just about inherent traits; it also involves cultivating learnable skills in the areas of assumptions, actions, communication, and appearance. By focusing on these four categories of skills, leaders can enhance their executive presence and become more effective in their roles. In the following chapters, we will explore practical strategies for developing these skills to improve executive presence.

Character, Substance, Style: The Three Dimensions of Executive Presence

Executive presence (EP) is more than just how you look or speak; it's about who you are as a leader. Character, substance, and style are three key dimensions of executive presence, each contributing to your overall impact and influence. In this chapter, we will explore these dimensions in detail, examining the ingredients that make up each and how they can be developed to enhance your executive presence.

1. Character

Character is the foundation of executive presence, representing your moral and ethical qualities. It's about how you conduct yourself, the values you uphold, and the integrity you demonstrate in your actions.

Ingredients of Character:

- ✓ Integrity: Acting in alignment with your values, even when faced with difficult decisions.
- ✓ Authenticity: Being true to yourself and others, and not pretending to be someone you're not.
- ✓ Honesty: Speaking truthfully and transparently in all your interactions.
- ✓ Resilience: Bouncing back from setbacks and remaining steadfast in your values.
- ✓ Empathy: Understanding and caring about the feelings and perspectives of others.
- ✓ Courage: Having the strength to do what is right, even in the face of adversity.

Real-Life Example:

John, a CEO, demonstrated exceptional character when he refused to compromise his company's values, even when pressured by stakeholders to do so. His integrity and courage in standing firm earned him the respect and trust of his team and stakeholders.

2. Substance

Substance refers to the depth and quality of your thoughts, ideas, and actions. It's about having substance behind your words and being able to back up your decisions with sound reasoning and expertise.

Ingredients of Substance:

- ✓ Strategic Thinking: Having a big-picture perspective and the ability to see long-term implications.
- ✓ Decisiveness: Making informed decisions in a timely manner, even when faced with uncertainty.
- ✓ Innovation: Thinking creatively and introducing new ideas and approaches.
- ✓ Expertise: Demonstrating a high level of knowledge and skill in your field.
- ✓ Vision: Articulating a clear and compelling vision for the future.
- ✓ Problem-Solving Skills: Being able to identify and address challenges effectively.

Real-Life Example:

Sarah, a senior executive, showed substance in her leadership by developing innovative solutions to complex problems faced by her team. Her ability to think strategically and find creative solutions set her apart as a leader with substance.

3. Style

Style refers to the way you present yourself and engage with others. It's about your communication style, demeanor, and overall approach to leadership.

Ingredients of Style:

- ✓ Communication Skills: Being able to convey your ideas clearly and persuasively.
- ✓ Presence: Projecting confidence and authority in your interactions.
- ✓ Listening Skills: Actively listening to others and showing empathy in your responses.
- ✓ Adaptability: Being able to adjust your communication style to suit different audiences.
- ✓ Emotional Intelligence: Understanding and managing your own emotions, as well as those of others.
- ✓ Networking Skills: Building and maintaining relationships with key stakeholders.

Real-Life Example:

Rachel, a leader, demonstrated effective style by communicating her vision clearly and engaging with her team in a way that motivated and inspired them. Her ability to adapt her communication style to different situations made her a highly effective communicator.

Character, substance, and style are integral components of executive presence, each contributing to your overall impact and influence as a leader. By developing these dimensions, you can enhance your executive presence and become a more effective leader in your organization. In the following chapters, we will explore practical strategies for developing each of these dimensions to enhance your executive presence.

Reflection Questions:

- ✓ Which characteristics of executive presence do you currently possess, and which ones do you need to develop further?
- ✓ Think of a leader you admire who exhibits strong executive presence. What specific traits do they possess that you can emulate?
- ✓ How do you believe your assumptions, actions, communication style, and appearance contribute to your overall executive presence?
- ✓ Reflect on a time when you observed someone with poor executive presence. What impact did it have on the situation or team?
- ✓ How can you enhance your executive presence through ongoing learning and development?

Part 3:
Authenticity, Grace, and Poise

The Power of Authenticity, Grace, and Poise in Executive Presence

Authenticity, grace, and poise are three qualities that can significantly enhance executive presence. In this chapter, we will explore how these qualities contribute to a leader's effectiveness and impact, using real-life examples to illustrate their importance.

1. Authenticity

- ✓ Authenticity is the alignment of one's words, actions, and values. Authentic leaders are genuine, transparent, and true to themselves, which builds trust and credibility with others.
- ✓ Example: Oprah Winfrey is known for her authenticity both on and off-screen. Her ability to openly share her struggles and triumphs has endeared her to audiences worldwide, making her a respected and influential figure.

2. Grace

- ✓ Grace is the ability to handle oneself with elegance, dignity, and tact in challenging situations. Leaders who possess grace remain calm under pressure and treat others with respect and empathy.
- ✓ Example: Nelson Mandela exemplified grace during his presidency in South Africa. Despite facing immense challenges and opposition, Mandela remained composed and focused on reconciliation, earning him respect and admiration globally.

3. Poise

- ✓ Poise is the ability to maintain a sense of balance and control, especially in difficult or high-pressure situations. Leaders with poise are able to think and act calmly, even in the face of adversity.

- ✓ Example: Michelle Obama is admired for her poise and grace as the former First Lady of the United States. Her ability to navigate the public spotlight with dignity and composure has made her a role model for many.

How Authenticity, Grace, and Poise Enhance Executive Presence

- ✓ **Build Trust:** Authenticity builds trust with others, as people are more likely to follow leaders who are genuine and true to themselves.
- ✓ **Inspire Confidence:** Grace and poise inspire confidence in others, as they demonstrate a leader's ability to remain calm and composed in challenging situations.
- ✓ **Foster Respect:** Leaders who exhibit authenticity, grace, and poise are respected for their ability to handle themselves with dignity and respect others.

Authenticity, grace, and poise are three qualities that can greatly enhance executive presence. By embodying these qualities, leaders can build trust, inspire confidence, and foster respect, ultimately becoming more effective and impactful in their roles.

The Impact of Authenticity, Grace, and Poise on Leadership Effectiveness

Authenticity, grace, and poise are not just individual attributes but also have a profound impact on leadership effectiveness, team dynamics, and organizational culture. In this chapter, we will explore how these qualities can influence various aspects of leadership and contribute to a positive work environment.

1. **Building Trust and Credibility**
   Authentic leaders are more likely to build trust and credibility with their teams and stakeholders. When leaders are genuine and true to themselves, they are perceived as more trustworthy, which fosters stronger relationships and loyalty.
   Example: A CEO who openly shares their values and principles with their team is more likely to be trusted and respected by their employees. This trust and credibility can lead to increased engagement and commitment from the team.
2. **Enhancing Communication and Collaboration**
   Grace and poise in communication can improve team dynamics and collaboration. Leaders who communicate with elegance and tact are more likely to resolve conflicts peacefully and inspire open and honest communication among team members.

Example: A leader who maintains their composure during a crisis can help calm the team and encourage constructive dialogue. This can lead to better problem-solving and decision-making within the team.

3. **Fostering a Positive Work Environment**
   Leaders who exhibit authenticity, grace, and poise contribute to a positive work environment. Their demeanor and behavior set the tone for the organization, influencing the culture and morale of the team.
   Example: A leader who shows empathy and understanding towards their team members creates a supportive work environment where employees feel valued and motivated to perform at their best.
4. **Inspiring Others**
   Authentic, graceful, and poised leaders are often seen as role models by their team members. Their behavior and actions inspire others to emulate their qualities, leading to a more cohesive and motivated team.
   Example: A leader who handles challenging situations with grace and poise inspires their team to approach difficulties with a similar mindset. This can lead to a more resilient and adaptable team that thrives in the face of adversity.

Authenticity, grace, and poise are not just personal attributes but also powerful leadership qualities that can positively impact leadership effectiveness, team dynamics, and organizational culture. By embodying these qualities, leaders can create a more trusting, collaborative, and positive work environment, ultimately leading to greater success for the team and the organization.

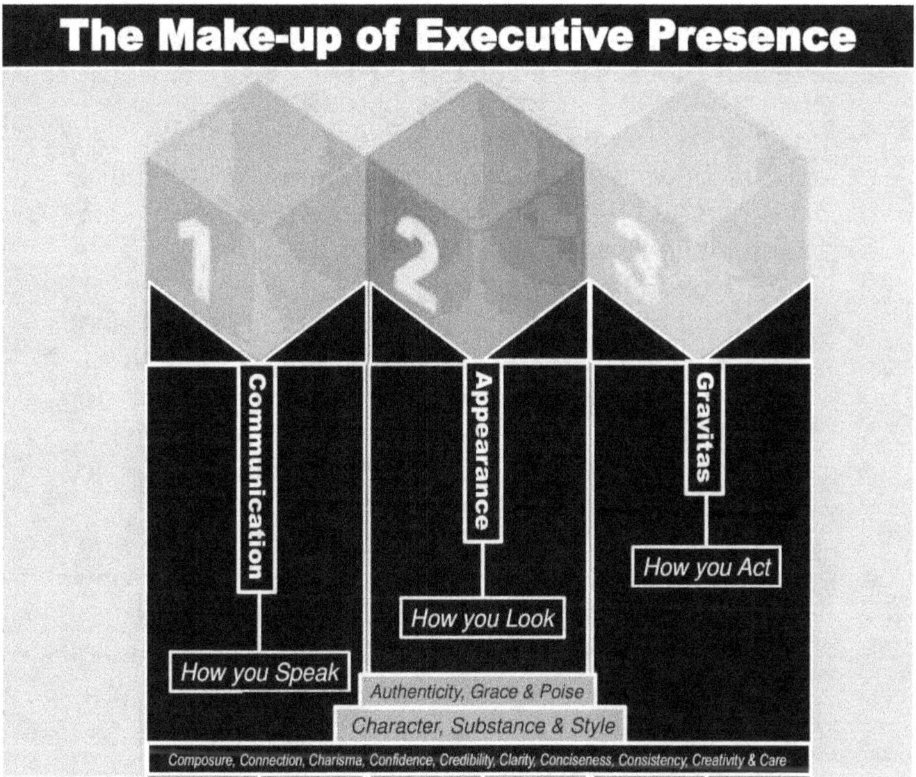

Authenticity as Alignment of Head, Mouth, Heart, and Feet

Authenticity is often described as the alignment of one's head (thoughts), mouth (words), heart (feelings), and feet (actions). When these elements are in harmony, a leader is perceived as genuine, trustworthy, and credible. In this chapter, we will explore how this alignment contributes to executive presence and leadership effectiveness, using real-life examples to illustrate its impact.

1. **Head (Thoughts)**
   Authenticity begins with clarity of thought and a strong sense of self-awareness. Leaders who are authentic in their thinking are able to articulate their values, beliefs, and vision clearly, which helps them stay true to themselves and inspire others.
   Example: Elon Musk, CEO of Tesla and SpaceX, is known for his visionary thinking and bold ideas. His ability to think outside the box and pursue his vision with unwavering conviction has earned him respect and admiration as an authentic leader.
2. **Mouth (Words)**
   Authentic leaders are mindful of their words and communicate with honesty and integrity. They speak with sincerity and transparency, avoiding empty promises or misleading statements.
   Example: Michelle Obama, former First Lady of the United States, is admired for her authenticity in speech. Her ability to connect with audiences through her genuine and

heartfelt words has made her a respected and influential figure.

3. **Heart (Feelings)**
   Authenticity is also about being in touch with one's emotions and being able to express them authentically. Leaders who lead with their hearts show empathy, compassion, and sincerity in their interactions with others.
   Example: Jacinda Ardern, Prime Minister of New Zealand, is praised for her compassionate leadership style. Her genuine concern for the well-being of her people, especially during times of crisis, has earned her widespread admiration and trust.
4. **Feet (Actions)**
   Authenticity is ultimately demonstrated through one's actions. Leaders who align their actions with their words and values inspire trust and confidence in their leadership.
   Example: Mahatma Gandhi, the leader of India's independence movement, is a timeless example of authentic leadership. His actions, such as leading nonviolent protests and living a simple life, were consistent with his beliefs and values.

Authenticity, as the alignment of head, mouth, heart, and feet, is a powerful force in leadership. Leaders who embody this alignment are able to inspire trust, build meaningful connections, and lead with integrity and purpose. By understanding and embracing the principles of authenticity, leaders can enhance their executive presence and make a lasting impact on their teams and organizations.

Reflection Questions

- ✓ How do authenticity, grace, and poise enhance your ability to lead and influence others?
- ✓ Reflect on a time when you demonstrated authenticity in a challenging situation. What was the outcome?
- ✓ How can you cultivate grace and poise in high-pressure or stressful environments?
- ✓ How do you ensure that your actions align with your values and beliefs, even in difficult circumstances?
- ✓ What steps will you take to further develop your authenticity, grace, and poise in your professional life?

Part 4:
Developing Executive Presence

Developing Executive Presence

Developing executive presence is a journey that requires self-awareness, practice, and a commitment to personal growth. In this chapter, we will outline a step-by-step plan using the principles discussed in earlier chapters to help you enhance your executive presence.

1. **Assess Your Current Level of Executive Presence**
   Before you can improve your executive presence, it's essential to understand where you currently stand. Use the self-assessment template provided in Chapter 16 to evaluate your strengths and areas for improvement.
2. **Define Your Personal Brand**
   Identify the key characteristics and values that you want to embody as a leader. Your personal brand should align with your authentic self and the qualities of executive presence discussed in Chapter 18.
   Example: Sarah, a marketing executive, defines her personal brand as innovative, empathetic, and decisive. She strives to demonstrate these qualities in her interactions with colleagues and clients.
3. **Enhance Your Communication Skills**
   Effective communication is a cornerstone of executive presence. Practice active listening, articulate your thoughts clearly, and use confident body language to convey your message.
   Example: John, a team leader, works on improving his communication skills by

participating in public speaking classes and seeking feedback from his peers.

4. **Cultivate Gravitas**
   Gravitas is about how you carry yourself and command respect. Develop a presence that is calm, confident, and authoritative, as discussed in Chapter 13.
   Example: Maria, a senior manager, cultivates gravitas by maintaining a composed demeanor in high-pressure situations and leading by example.
5. **Project Authenticity, Grace, and Poise**
   Authenticity, grace, and poise are key elements of executive presence. Stay true to yourself, handle challenges with elegance, and remain composed under pressure.
   Example: James, a CEO, demonstrates authenticity by being transparent with his team and showing empathy towards their concerns.
6. **Seek Feedback and Adjust**
   Regularly seek feedback from colleagues, mentors, and trusted advisors to assess your progress and make adjustments as needed.
   Example: Laura, a director, regularly solicits feedback from her team to ensure that her leadership style aligns with their needs and expectations.

Developing executive presence is a continuous process that requires dedication and self-reflection. By following this step-by-step plan and incorporating the principles discussed in earlier chapters, you can enhance your executive presence and become a more effective leader.

A Step-by-Step Action Plan with Checklists for Developing Executive Presence

Step 1: Self-Assessment

- ✓ **Objective:** Understand your current level of executive presence and identify areas for improvement.
- ✓ **Action Items:**
  Use the self-assessment template provided in Chapter 16 to evaluate your strengths and weaknesses.
  Reflect on feedback from colleagues, mentors, and supervisors.
- ✓ **Checklist:**
  Completed self-assessment.
  Feedback from others.

Step 2: Define Your Personal Brand

- ✓ **Objective:** Define the key characteristics and values you want to embody as a leader.
- ✓ **Action Items:**
  Identify your unique strengths, values, and goals.
  Determine how you want to be perceived by others.
- ✓ **Checklist:**
  Defined personal brand statement.
  List of key characteristics and values.

Step 3: Enhance Your Communication Skills

- ✓ **Objective:** Improve your ability to communicate effectively and confidently.
- ✓ **Action Items:**
  Attend communication workshops or classes.

Practice active listening and assertive communication.

- ✓ **Checklist:**

  Attended communication training.

  Practiced active listening and assertiveness.

Step 4: Cultivate Gravitas

- ✓ **Objective:** Develop a presence that commands respect and authority.
- ✓ **Action Items:**

  Practice maintaining composure in challenging situations.

  Seek opportunities to lead by example.
- ✓ **Checklist:**

  Demonstrated composure in challenging situations.

  Led by example in at least one instance.

Step 5: Project Authenticity, Grace, and Poise

- ✓ **Objective:** Demonstrate authenticity, grace, and poise in your interactions.
- ✓ **Action Items:**

  Practice being genuine and transparent in your communication.

  Handle challenging situations with grace and poise.
- ✓ **Checklist:**

  Demonstrated authenticity in communication.

  Handled challenging situations with grace.

Step 6: Seek Feedback and Adjust

- ✓ **Objective:** Regularly seek feedback to assess your progress and make adjustments.
- ✓ **Action Items:**

  Request feedback from colleagues, mentors, and supervisors.

Use feedback to identify areas for improvement and adjust your actions accordingly.

✓ **Checklist:**
Received feedback from multiple sources.
Implemented changes based on feedback.

Step 7: Maintain and Enhance Your Executive Presence

✓ **Objective:** Continuously work on maintaining and enhancing your executive presence.

✓ **Action Items:**
Regularly revisit your personal brand and goals.
Continue to seek opportunities for growth and development.

✓ **Checklist:**
Reviewed and updated personal brand statement.
Continued professional development activities.

By following this step-by-step action plan and using the checklists provided, you can systematically work on developing your executive presence. Remember that developing executive presence is a continuous journey, and it requires ongoing effort and self-reflection.

Developing Executive Presence: Exercises and Activities for Practice

Developing executive presence requires more than just understanding the concept; it also involves practical application and continuous practice. In this chapter, we will explore a variety of exercises and activities that you can use to enhance your executive presence in real-life situations.

1. Communication Skills

- ✓ *Exercise:* Record Yourself Speaking
- ✓ Objective: Improve your speaking skills and identify areas for improvement.
- ✓ How to: Record yourself giving a short presentation or speaking on a topic. Watch the recording and assess your tone, pace, and clarity of speech. Look for areas where you can improve.

2. Body Language

- ✓ *Exercise:* Power Pose
- ✓ Objective: Boost your confidence and presence through body language.
- ✓ How to: Stand in a "power pose" for two minutes before a meeting or presentation. This could be standing with your feet shoulder-width apart, hands on hips, and chin up. Studies suggest that adopting power poses can increase feelings of confidence and dominance.

3. Authenticity

- ✓ *Activity:* Values Alignment
- ✓ Objective: Align your actions with your values to project authenticity.

- ✓ How to: Identify your core values and reflect on how you can demonstrate them in your daily interactions. For example, if one of your values is honesty, consider how you can be more transparent in your communication.

4. Gravitas

- ✓ *Activity:* Leadership Presence Observation
- ✓ Objective: Observe leaders with strong gravitas and learn from their behavior.
- ✓ How to: Attend a meeting or watch a video of a leader known for their gravitas. Take note of how they carry themselves, their demeanor, and their interactions with others. Try to emulate some of these behaviors in your own leadership style.

5. Poise Under Pressure

- ✓ *Exercise:* Stress Management Techniques
- ✓ Objective: Develop strategies to maintain poise under pressure.
- ✓ How to: Practice stress management techniques such as deep breathing, mindfulness, or visualization. Use these techniques before and during stressful situations to help you stay calm and composed.

6. Feedback and Reflection

- ✓ *Exercise:* Feedback Journal
- ✓ Objective: Gather feedback from others and reflect on your progress.
- ✓ How to: Keep a journal where you write down feedback you receive from colleagues, mentors, or supervisors. Reflect on this feedback regularly and identify areas where you can improve.

By engaging in these exercises and activities, you can actively work on developing your executive presence and enhance your leadership skills. Remember that executive presence is not something that can be developed overnight; it requires consistent effort and practice.

Tips for Maintaining and Enhancing Executive Presence over Time

Developing executive presence is a continuous process that requires ongoing effort and self-reflection. In this chapter, we will explore some tips and strategies to help you maintain and enhance your executive presence over time, ensuring that you continue to project confidence, credibility, and authority in your leadership role.

1. **Continuously Refine Your Personal Brand**
   Your personal brand is a reflection of who you are as a leader. Continuously refine and update your personal brand to ensure that it aligns with your current goals and values.
   Example: Emily, a marketing director, regularly updates her personal brand statement to reflect her evolving leadership style and career aspirations. By staying true to her values and goals, she maintains a strong and consistent personal brand.
2. **Seek Regular Feedback**
   Feedback is essential for growth and development. Seek feedback from colleagues, mentors, and supervisors on a regular basis to identify areas for improvement and make adjustments accordingly.
   Example: David, a project manager, regularly solicits feedback from his team on his leadership style and communication skills. By actively seeking feedback, he is able to address any issues and continuously improve his executive presence.
3. **Stay Current and Informed**

Stay informed about industry trends, developments, and best practices to ensure that you remain relevant and knowledgeable in your field. This will help you project confidence and credibility in your interactions.

Example: Sarah, a finance executive, subscribes to industry publications and attends conferences to stay updated on the latest trends and developments in finance. This enables her to engage in informed discussions and demonstrate her expertise in her field.

4. **Practice Active Listening**

   Effective communication is key to executive presence. Practice active listening by fully engaging with others and demonstrating empathy and understanding in your interactions.

   Example: John, a senior executive, practices active listening by maintaining eye contact, nodding, and paraphrasing what others say. This helps him build rapport and demonstrate his genuine interest in others' perspectives.

5. **Maintain a Professional Appearance**

   Your appearance plays a significant role in how others perceive you. Maintain a professional appearance by dressing appropriately for your role and maintaining good grooming habits.

   Example: Laura, a CEO, pays attention to her appearance by wearing well-fitted suits and ensuring her hair and makeup are neat and professional. This helps her project a polished and professional image in her leadership role.

By following these tips and strategies, you can maintain and enhance your executive presence over time, ensuring that you continue to inspire confidence, credibility, and respect as a leader. Remember that executive presence is not a static trait but a dynamic quality that requires continuous effort and attention.

Identifying Areas for Improvement and Providing/Receiving Feedback

Self-awareness is a critical component of executive presence. In this chapter, we will explore strategies for identifying areas for improvement and effectively giving and receiving feedback to enhance your executive presence.

1. **Self-Reflection and Assessment**
   Self-reflection is key to identifying areas for improvement. Take time to reflect on your interactions, behaviors, and leadership style to pinpoint areas where you can enhance your executive presence.
   Example: Alex, a sales manager, regularly sets aside time for self-reflection to assess his performance in client meetings. By analyzing his communication style and client interactions, he identifies areas where he can improve his executive presence.
2. **Seek Feedback from Others**
   Feedback from others is invaluable for growth and development. Seek feedback from colleagues, mentors, and supervisors to gain insights into how you are perceived and identify areas for improvement.
   Example: Sarah, a marketing executive, regularly seeks feedback from her team on her leadership style and communication skills. By listening to their perspectives, she gains valuable insights into areas where she can enhance her executive presence.
3. **Provide Constructive Feedback**

Providing constructive feedback to others is also an important skill. When providing feedback, focus on specific behaviors and their impact, and offer suggestions for improvement.

Example: David, a project manager, provides constructive feedback to his team members on their presentation skills. By offering specific examples and actionable advice, he helps them improve their executive presence.

4. **Receiving Feedback Gracefully**

   Receiving feedback gracefully is essential for growth. Listen attentively, thank the person for their feedback, and reflect on how you can use it to enhance your executive presence.

   Example: Laura, a CEO, receives feedback from her board members on her leadership style. She listens carefully to their input, acknowledges their perspectives, and considers how she can improve her executive presence.

5. **Implementing Feedback**

   Implementing feedback is crucial for growth. Identify specific actions you can take to address areas for improvement and commit to making changes.

   Example: John, a senior executive, receives feedback on his communication style. He decides to enroll in a public speaking course to improve his presentation skills and enhance his executive presence.

By actively seeking feedback, both from yourself and others, and implementing changes based on that feedback, you can continuously improve your executive presence. Remember that feedback is a gift that can help you grow and develop as a leader.

Executive Presence in Virtual Settings

In today's digital age, virtual meetings and remote work are becoming increasingly common. As a leader, it's essential to maintain your executive presence even in virtual settings. In this chapter, we will explore strategies for projecting confidence, credibility, and authority in virtual meetings.

1. **Setting the Stage**
   Creating a professional and conducive virtual environment is key to projecting executive presence. Pay attention to your background, lighting, and camera angle to ensure you appear professional on screen.
   Example: Maria, a senior executive, always ensures she has a clean and professional background during virtual meetings. She also invests in good lighting to ensure she is clearly visible to participants.
2. **Engaging Body Language**
   Body language plays a crucial role in virtual meetings. Maintain good posture, make eye contact with the camera, and use gestures to emphasize your points.
   Example: Mark, a team leader, uses hand gestures to convey enthusiasm and engagement during virtual meetings. This helps him maintain a strong presence even in a digital environment.
3. **Effective Communication**
   Clear and concise communication is essential in virtual settings. Use a confident tone of

voice, speak clearly, and avoid talking too quickly.

Example: Sarah, a project manager, practices speaking slowly and clearly during virtual meetings to ensure her message is understood. This helps her maintain authority and credibility.

4. **Active Listening**

   Active listening is just as important in virtual meetings as it is in face-to-face interactions. Show that you are engaged by nodding, using verbal cues, and asking clarifying questions.

   Example: John, a sales executive, demonstrates active listening during virtual meetings by nodding and using phrases like "I see" or "That makes sense." This helps him build rapport with colleagues and clients.

5. **Managing Technology**

   Technical issues can disrupt your executive presence in virtual meetings. Familiarize yourself with the technology and troubleshoot any potential issues before the meeting.

   Example: Laura, a CEO, always tests her audio and video settings before joining a virtual meeting. This ensures she can confidently lead the meeting without technical interruptions.

6. **Leading with Confidence**

   Despite the virtual setting, it's important to lead with confidence and authority. Be prepared, stay focused, and maintain a positive attitude throughout the meeting.

   Example: David, a team manager, leads virtual meetings with confidence by setting a clear agenda and guiding the discussion. This helps him maintain control and authority in the virtual space.

Conclusion

By applying these strategies, you can enhance your executive presence in virtual settings and effectively lead and communicate with your team. Remember, even in a digital world, your presence and leadership impact can shine through with the right approach.

Do's and Don'ts for Virtual Meetings:

Do's for Virtual Meetings:

- ✓ **Do:** Dress professionally from head to toe, even if only your upper half is visible on camera.
- ✓ **Do:** Test your audio and video equipment before the meeting to ensure clear communication.
- ✓ **Do:** Maintain good posture and make eye contact with the camera to convey confidence and engagement.
- ✓ **Do:** Use clear and concise language to communicate your points effectively.
- ✓ **Do:** Engage in active listening by nodding and providing verbal cues to show you are attentive.
- ✓ **Do:** Use appropriate hand gestures and facial expressions to emphasize your points.
- ✓ **Do:** Be prepared for the meeting with an agenda and any necessary materials.
- ✓ **Do:** Manage your time effectively to keep the meeting on track and respect others' time.
- ✓ **Do:** Encourage participation from all attendees and create a welcoming environment for discussion.

- ✓ **Do:** Follow up after the meeting with a summary of key points and action items.

Don'ts for Virtual Meetings:

- ✓ **Don't:** Dress too casually, even if you are working from home.
- ✓ **Don't:** Use distracting backgrounds or lighting that can detract from your message.
- ✓ **Don't:** Interrupt or talk over others; wait for your turn to speak.
- ✓ **Don't:** Allow yourself to be distracted by emails, messages, or other notifications during the meeting.
- ✓ **Don't:** Use jargon or technical language that may not be understood by all attendees.
- ✓ **Don't:** Speak too quickly or softly; ensure your voice is clear and audible.
- ✓ **Don't:** Slouch or appear disinterested; maintain an attentive and engaged posture.
- ✓ **Don't:** Monopolize the conversation; allow others to share their thoughts and ideas.
- ✓ **Don't:** Forget to follow up on action items or commitments made during the meeting.
- ✓ **Don't:** Be overly critical or dismissive of others' ideas; maintain a respectful and positive tone.

Reflection Questions:

- ✓ What specific actions can you take to enhance your composure, connection, and charisma in professional settings?
- ✓ How can you improve your confidence and credibility when interacting with colleagues, clients, or stakeholders?

- ✓ Reflect on a recent presentation or meeting. What feedback would you give yourself in terms of clarity and conciseness?
- ✓ How do you plan to maintain and enhance your executive presence over time?
- ✓ What role does continuous learning and self-improvement play in developing your executive presence?

Part 5:
Commanding Respect like a CEO

Commanding Respect like a CEO

Commanding respect is an essential aspect of executive presence, especially for senior leaders. In this chapter, we will explore strategies for projecting confidence, authority, and respect in various professional settings.

1. **Displaying Confidence in Meetings**
   Confidence is key to commanding respect. Project confidence in meetings by speaking clearly, making eye contact, and expressing your ideas with conviction.
   Example: Michael, a senior executive, displays confidence in meetings by speaking calmly and confidently, even when faced with challenging questions or situations. His demeanor commands respect from his colleagues and subordinates.
2. **Delivering Impactful Presentations**
   Presentations offer a platform to showcase your knowledge and expertise. Deliver impactful presentations by preparing thoroughly, engaging your audience, and delivering your message with clarity and conviction.
   Example: Sarah, a marketing director, delivers impactful presentations by using visuals, storytelling, and real-life examples to illustrate her points. Her presentations are not only informative but also inspiring, commanding respect from her audience.
3. **Building Your Network**
   Networking is essential for building relationships and gaining influence. Build your

network by attending industry events, connecting with professionals in your field, and actively engaging with your peers and colleagues.

Example: John, a business development manager, builds his network by attending networking events and conferences. His proactive approach to networking has helped him build valuable connections and gain respect in his industry.

4. **Leading with Authority**

   Leadership is about inspiring others to follow your vision. Lead with authority by setting clear goals, making informed decisions, and taking decisive action when necessary.

7. *Example:* Laura, a CEO, leads with authority by setting a clear vision for her company and empowering her team to achieve their goals. Her strong leadership style commands respect from her employees and stakeholders.

By following these strategies, you can command respect like a CEO and enhance your executive presence in professional settings. Remember, respect is earned through your actions, demeanor, and ability to lead with confidence and authority.

Displaying Confidence in Meetings

Confidence is a key component of executive presence, particularly in meetings where your ability to lead and influence others is on display. In this chapter, we will explore strategies for displaying confidence in meetings and provide a list of do's and don'ts to help you enhance your executive presence.

1. **Preparing for the Meeting**
   Preparation is crucial for displaying confidence in meetings. Familiarize yourself with the agenda, objectives, and participants beforehand to ensure you are well-informed and ready to contribute.
   Example: Before a board meeting, Alex spends time reviewing the meeting agenda and preparing his talking points. This preparation helps him feel more confident and articulate during the meeting.
2. **Body Language**
   Body language can convey confidence or nervousness. Maintain good posture, make eye contact, and use gestures to emphasize your points and engage with others.
   Example: Sarah sits up straight and makes eye contact with colleagues during a team meeting. Her confident body language helps her command attention and respect from others.
3. **Speaking with Clarity and Conviction**
   When speaking in meetings, articulate your thoughts clearly and confidently. Avoid using filler words or uncertain language that may undermine your message.

Example: John delivers a presentation to senior leadership with clarity and conviction. His confident speaking style helps him convey his ideas effectively and gain buy-in from the team.

4. **Active Listening**
   Active listening is a sign of confidence and respect for others' opinions. Listen attentively, ask clarifying questions, and show genuine interest in what others have to say.
   Example: Laura demonstrates active listening in a strategy meeting by nodding and taking notes while colleagues speak. Her attentive listening helps her contribute thoughtfully to the discussion.

Do's and Don'ts of Displaying Confidence in Meetings

Do's:

- ✓ Do prepare thoroughly for the meeting.
- ✓ Do maintain good posture and eye contact.
- ✓ Do speak clearly and confidently.
- ✓ Do listen actively and engage with others.
- ✓ Do contribute thoughtfully to the discussion.

Don'ts:

- ✓ Don't slouch or appear disinterested.
- ✓ Don't interrupt others; wait for your turn to speak.
- ✓ Don't use filler words or uncertain language.
- ✓ Don't dominate the conversation; allow others to share their ideas.
- ✓ Don't be afraid to ask questions or seek clarification.

By following these strategies and guidelines, you can display confidence in meetings and enhance your executive presence. Remember, confidence is not just about what you say, but how you say it and how you engage with others in a professional setting.

Delivering Impactful Presentations

Presentations are a powerful tool for showcasing your knowledge, expertise, and leadership skills. In this chapter, we will explore strategies for delivering impactful presentations that command attention and leave a lasting impression.

1. **Preparing Your Presentation**
   Effective preparation is the foundation of a successful presentation. Define your objective, structure your content logically, and tailor your message to your audience's needs and expectations.
   Example: Emily, a marketing manager, prepares for a product launch presentation by researching her target market, organizing her key points, and rehearsing her delivery. Her thorough preparation helps her deliver a compelling presentation that resonates with her audience.
2. **Engaging Your Audience**
   Engaging your audience is key to delivering an impactful presentation. Use storytelling, visuals, and interactive elements to capture their attention and keep them engaged throughout your presentation.
   Example: James, a sales director, begins his sales pitch with a compelling story that illustrates the benefits of his product. He uses visuals and real-life examples to engage his audience and make his presentation more memorable.
3. **Delivering Your Message with Clarity and Conviction**

The way you deliver your message is as important as the content itself. Speak clearly, use confident body language, and maintain eye contact with your audience to convey your message with conviction.

Example: Rachel, a project manager, delivers a project update presentation with confidence and clarity. Her strong delivery style helps her convey complex information in a way that is easy for her audience to understand.

4. **Handling Questions and Feedback**

   Be prepared to handle questions and feedback from your audience. Listen carefully, provide thoughtful responses, and use questions as an opportunity to further engage with your audience.

   Example: David, a business consultant, responds to questions from his audience with confidence and expertise. He uses questions to clarify his points and demonstrate his knowledge, earning the respect and trust of his audience.

Do's & Don'ts for Making an Impactful Presentation and Demonstrating Executive Presence

Do's

- ✓ Do prepare thoroughly for your presentation.
- ✓ Do: Start with a strong opening to grab the audience's attention.
- ✓ Do: Use visuals and storytelling to make your presentation engaging.
- ✓ Do: Speak clearly and confidently, using varied tones and gestures.

- ✓ Do: Maintain eye contact with your audience to establish rapport.
- ✓ Do: Dress professionally to convey authority and credibility.
- ✓ Do: Use confident body language, such as standing tall and using open gestures.
- ✓ Do: Practice your presentation to ensure smooth delivery and timing.
- ✓ Do: Be prepared to handle questions and feedback with grace and professionalism.
- ✓ Do: Follow up after the presentation to reinforce key points and thank the audience.

Don'ts

- ✓ Don't forget to practice your delivery and timing before the presentation.
- ✓ Don't: Read from your slides; use them as visual aids to support your message.
- ✓ Don't: Speak too quickly or softly; ensure your voice is clear and audible.
- ✓ Don't: Use filler words or uncertain language; speak with confidence and conviction.
- ✓ Don't: Slouch or appear disinterested; maintain an engaged and attentive posture.
- ✓ Don't: Overwhelm your audience with too much information; keep your presentation focused and concise.
- ✓ Don't: Ignore questions or feedback; address them respectfully and thoughtfully.
- ✓ Don't: Forget to tailor your presentation to your audience's needs and interests.
- ✓ Don't: Rush through your presentation; take your time to emphasize key points and allow for audience engagement.

- ✓ Don't: Forget to smile and show enthusiasm for your topic; your passion will help captivate your audience.

By following these strategies and guidelines, you can deliver impactful presentations that command attention and leave a lasting impression on your audience. Remember, the key to a successful presentation is not just what you say, but how you say it and how you engage with your audience.

Building a Strong Network

Building a strong network is essential for professional success and demonstrating executive presence. In this chapter, we will explore strategies for building and maintaining a strong network, along with real-life examples and stories to illustrate these concepts.

Importance of Networking

- ✓ Networking is not just about making connections; it's about building relationships that can help you advance in your career. A strong network can provide support, advice, and opportunities for growth.
- ✓ *Example:* Jessica, a marketing manager, attributes much of her career success to her strong network. Through networking events and industry conferences, she has built relationships with key influencers and decision-makers, which has opened doors to new opportunities and collaborations.

Strategies for Building Your Network

- ✓ Attend Networking Events: Attend industry events, conferences, and seminars to meet new people and expand your network.
- ✓ Utilize Social Media: Use platforms like LinkedIn to connect with professionals in your field and engage with industry-related content.
- ✓ Join Professional Associations: Joining associations related to your industry can provide networking opportunities and access to valuable resources.
- ✓ Volunteer for Leadership Roles: Volunteering for leadership roles in professional

organizations can help you build credibility and expand your network.

Maintaining and Nurturing Your Network

- ✓ Building a network is not enough; you must also maintain and nurture it. Stay in touch with your contacts, offer help and support when needed, and be proactive in seeking opportunities to connect.
- ✓ *Example:* Mark, a sales executive, makes it a point to regularly check in with his network contacts. Whether it's sending a congratulatory email on a recent achievement or sharing an article of interest, he ensures that he stays on their radar and maintains a strong relationship.

Leveraging Your Network

- ✓ Your network can be a valuable resource for career development. Use your network to seek advice, gather information, and explore new opportunities.
- ✓ *Example:* Sarah, a human resources manager, was able to find a new job through her network. A former colleague referred her to an opening at their company, highlighting the importance of maintaining strong relationships even after leaving a job.

Do's and Don'ts of Networking

Do's:

- ✓ Do be genuine and authentic in your interactions.
- ✓ Do follow up with contacts after networking events.
- ✓ Do offer help and support to your network contacts.

- ✓ Do be proactive in seeking out networking opportunities.

Don'ts:

- ✓ Don't be overly aggressive or pushy in your networking efforts.
- ✓ Don't only reach out to your network when you need something.
- ✓ Don't forget to thank people for their time and assistance.
- ✓ Don't limit your networking efforts to only those in your immediate field or industry.

By following these strategies and guidelines, you can build a strong network that will not only support your career growth but also enhance your executive presence. Networking is an ongoing process, so continue to nurture and expand your network throughout your career.

Reflection Questions:

- ✓ How do you currently command respect in your professional interactions? What areas do you need to improve?
- ✓ Reflect on a time when you successfully displayed confidence in a meeting or presentation. What strategies did you use?
- ✓ What are some common pitfalls to avoid when trying to demonstrate executive presence?
- ✓ How can you build and expand your professional network to enhance your influence and impact?
- ✓ What steps will you take to ensure that you consistently project confidence and authority in your role?

Part 6:
Maintaining Professionalism: Conclusion

Maintaining Professionalism: Positive First Impressions and More!

Managing You-Positive First Impressions!

Have you ever wondered about the impressions you could create even before you open our mouth?

In a study carried out that I am about to share with you now, you will notice that people place more emphasis on what they SEE rather than on what they HEAR. So this only tells us that we need to be very careful with our body language and what we are projecting.

According to studies carried out, Communication takes place in 3 forms:

- ✓ Your Words
- ✓ Your Tone and
- ✓ Your Body Language.

Where 55% has to do with your Body Language or what others 'See'

7 % has to do with 'What' you say or your words

Whilst 38% has to do with 'How' those words are said, which is your Tone or voice modulation

With people going by what they SEE first rather than what they HEAR, it makes it very important for us to therefore project the RIGHT image upfront. That's the first impression that has been formed-good or bad! If it is good, then very good for you, but if it is bad, then so sad! Because...now you have double work to undo the wrong impression that has already gone into the mind and to now fill it with the right impression.

They say 90% of lasting impressions are created in the first 90 seconds. That can be really dangerous, but surprisingly that is true! So we have to be very careful, with what are we projecting as soon as someone sees us, because that's what they will remember.

It is also a reason why we tend to remember a song seen on a television set better than when heard through a radio. The same logic applies at a job interview with your resume and the presentation of it! Then at the interview-the interviewer has made up his mind to a great extent as you walk in, even before you have opened your mouth. Your bio-profile or the interview process is only a confirmation of the decision already made in the mind of the interviewer.

Why is Tone next important after Body Language? Simply because you can say a same sentence with a different tone and that can change the entire meaning

Eg; "Mary come here" is a simple sentence. But depending on the right tone, this one sentence could turn out as an 'order 'or a 'request'.

Another stronger example: "Hang him not let him go"...could be death or life depending on how it is said. Example: 'Hang him, not let him go'! Or 'Hang him not, let him go'!

Now, if it is face to face, we may be able to save the situation, but when on the phone with the other person not able to see you, it could lead to miscommunication if the right tone is not used.

As seen earlier, with people going by what they 'See' first rather than what they 'Hear', it makes it so very important for us to therefore project the RIGHT image upfront. It basically involves Selling Yourself first!

Before a customer buys anything or decides to do business with you or the company that you represent, he needs to first be sold on you because you are what he sees about your company to him. Your company could have a several floor building, with several offices all across the globe. But to the person doing business with you, what he sees in you is the impression he has formed of your company! Because…90% of lasting impressions are created in the first 90 seconds

A person forms an impression of you, usually in less than ten seconds, based on a combination of some of these attributes:

Posture, Walk
Body language
Attire, Clothing
Physical characteristics
Smile, Facial features
Handshake
Cleanliness, Grooming
Scent, perfume
Eye contact
Perceived Confidence

In a study, men and women were asked to list the attributes they found attractive and unattractive in someone they met. And here is the list of some of the top responses:

Qualities that create a Positive Impression:

- ✓ Warmth
- ✓ Sense of humor
- ✓ Imagination
- ✓ Fitness
- ✓ Individuality
- ✓ Positive body language
- ✓ Conversational ability
- ✓ Creativity

- ✓ Kindness

Qualities that create a Negative Impression
- ✓ Self-centered
- ✓ Closed minded
- ✓ Judgmental
- ✓ Lack of manners
- ✓ Poor conversational ability
- ✓ Negative attitude
- ✓ Indecisiveness
- ✓ Lack of integrity
- ✓ Complaining and whining
- ✓ Politics and Power games
- ✓ Manipulation

Making a Great First Impression
If you want to make a good impression, know that you need to project **3 C's:**
- ✓ Confidence
- Have a straight but relaxed posture. Hold your head high and steady. Don't slouch or slump.
- Move in a natural, unaffected manner.
- Maintain eye contact with the people you are talking to.
- ✓ Competence
- Exhibit your knowledge when required. Know your way around the agenda. Be prepared for the meeting. Bring supportive materials to emphasize your points.
- Answer questions in a clear and professional manner, avoiding the use of slang or technical jargon.
- Ask relevant questions if needed.
- ✓ Credibility
- Arrive on time.

- Be presentable (well-groomed and mindful of dress codes)
- Keep true to your word.
- When uncertain, err on the side of what you presume is conservatism. And be observant; check if people are becoming uncomfortable.
- Etiquette mishaps can range from merely embarrassing to potentially insulting to the other person. When you realize that you have committed a faux pas, apologize immediately and ask how you can make up for it

Appearance IS Everything! It starts with your Personal Grooming

Paying attention to your grooming by taking care of your cleanliness and your clothing demonstrates respect for yourself and for others- the key words being neat and clean.

- ✓ A general rule of thumb is: the more expensive the products/services you sell, the more professional you should look-Customers make assumptions about you based on your appearance.
- ✓ If it's an expensive product you are selling, the customer is bound to think: "How can this person help us make this expensive purchase when he can't even afford a proper wardrobe and take care of himself?"

Projecting the Right Image!

- ✓ How you dress, how you groom yourself and how you handle yourself in public is all part of your "packaging"
- ✓ Like product packaging, you can present yourself to be most appealing. And, you can

present yourself differently according to the time and place.

- ✓ Presence is how you "present" yourself- it's your self-confidence, poise and appeal.

So what does it take to make a Special, Positive, and Instant Impression when prospective 'buyers' first see you.

According to Drew Westen, in his fabulous book "The Political Brain" one of the main determinants of electoral success," he explains, "is simply a candidate's curb appeal". Curb appeal is the feeling voters get when they 'drive by' a candidate a few times on television and form an emotional impression! Personal Curb Appeal is primarily a nonverbal process.

How's your Personal Curb Appeal? When your co-workers, clients, and business partners "drive by" you, how do you come across? Here are a few tips to keep in mind:

- ✓ Dress for success: Always dress and see yourself for the next level!
- ✓ Your motto should be: "Wear great clothes. You never know whom you'll meet!" When it comes to curb appeal, the way you dress matters. Clothing has an effect on both the observer and the wearer.
- ✓ Dressing for success doesn't necessarily mean you have to wear a suit to work. Many organizations have a more casual dress code. But it does mean that whatever you wear should help you make the statement that you are a competent professional.

The finest clothing made is a person's skin, but, of course, society demands something more than this- Mark Twain

Wardrobe Management

Your dress is either working for you or against you. Clothes send a message about how you want others to see you. The way you dress can play a big role in your professional career. Part of the culture of a company is the dress code of its employees. Some companies prefer a business casual approach, while other companies require a business professional dress code.

These guidelines provided, are only suggestions, as you would need to always research the event, function, occasion or environment in question to determine the appropriate dress attire. Each industry-professional, community, and academic, may sometimes follow its own wardrobe standards and traditions.

But remember: If you are not too sure when business casual is appropriate, then always remember the general rule of thumb: *It's better to be over-dressed, than under-dressed.*

Professional Dressing:

Business attire suggests formal, conservative dress style. Attention to detail, impeccable grooming, and a well-fitting suit are vital to make a good lasting impression.

The Suit: Choose a classic, neutral suit in charcoal, black, grey or navy. Avoid suits that conform to trends. Best fabrics for suits are wool/wool blends which can be worn all year and do not wrinkle easily. Skirt suits are appropriate feminine attire as long as the skirt hits or covers the knee and there are no large slits at the side, front, or back. The pant leg should touch the front of the shoe and fall just above the heel in the back. Make sure the suit flatters your body type and fits well, not too tight or loose.

The Dress Shirt: Choose shirts in a pale, subtle color (i.e., blue, cream, white, baby pink). Long sleeved, button-up shirts are most appropriate. Your shirt sleeve should extend beyond the suit jacket sleeves by half an inch. Pointed collars give a more professional image than button-down collars, yet both are acceptable. Choose shirts with more cotton than polyester; they resist wrinkling.

Shoes/Socks/Belt/Accessories etc:

Shoes: Leather in lace-ups shoes and should not be lighter than the trouser color. Shoes that match your suit or are slightly darker are the best choice in colors, such as brown, black, tan, or navy. The shoe should have a real sole (no sneakers, sandals, or street shoes) and a closed toe. Avoid platforms and heels higher than 2 inches. Shoes should be polished and in good condition. Wear black shoes with grey, navy or black suits and dark brown shoes with tan, brown or beige suits.

Socks: Preferable 100% cotton in black, brown, grey or navy. Choose a color to match or blend with trousers. Be sure to wear socks that cover your calves.

Ties: Tie and suit color should complement each other, but not match. Burgundy, red and navy blue work as good background colors. Small geometric prints and stripes are good choices. Paisleys with subdued patterns are alternatives. Silk ties are the preferred choice. They are elegant and can be worn all year in any climate. The tie knot should fill the space at the top of the shirt. Do not wear a matching handkerchief/ pocket square.

Belts: Either leather or reptile in black, brown or burgundy. Use discreet brass or good metal buckles. Suspenders are acceptable. Belts should be in good condition and match the color of your shoes, avoiding fancy and flashy buckles.

Briefcases: Briefcase should ideally be brown, black or burgundy leather, matching your shoes

Accessories: Jewellery ideally should be no more than one ring per hand. Good quality watches. No earring or studs for men

The right business attire never includes the following:

- ✓ Jeans (of any color)
- ✓ Athletic wear (e.g. sweat suits)
- ✓ Leggings
- ✓ T-shirts
- ✓ Low-cut garments, front or back
- ✓ Any kind of workout clothes, running or gym shoes, sneakers or sandals
- ✓ Hats, caps
- ✓ Ripped or tattered clothing
- ✓ Extremely tight-fitting clothes

What to keep in mind when buying your garments?

Before making a purchase, men and women need to answer "yes" to these key questions. If you are in doubt, don't buy the item, as clothes should look and feel good.

- ✓ Did you try the garment on?
- ✓ Did you check the fit in the front and the back?

- ✓ Is the suit jacket long enough to cover the buttocks?
- ✓ Are the button holes sewn tightly?
- ✓ Can you move around freely in the garment?
- ✓ Does the product feel comfortable?
- ✓ Check for pulls, bulges or bunching of the material.
- ✓ Do you like the garment? Buy a garment because you like it, not just to add to your wardrobe

How to Wear a Blazer or Suit

When planning to wear a blazer or a suit, here are a few tips on using them the right way. The first thing that you might want to consider when wearing a men's suit is how many buttons it will have. Although this may seem insignificant, the truth is that it is very important.

- ✓ When you wear a 3-button suit, you will button the top or top two buttons.
- ✓ When you wear a 2-button suit, you will button only the top button.
- ✓ With a 4-button suit, it is typically acceptable to button the two middle buttons, leaving the top button and the bottom button undone
- ✓ With a double-breasted suit, all buttons are buttoned.

When wearing a suit or Blazer:

- ✓ If you are seated, your suit coat should always be open. It is not acceptable to take off your suit coat unless you are to be seated for an extended period of time, like for a meal, or in your office, or if your host does so, etc.

- ✓ If you wish to take your suit coat off in company, it is polite to ask permission (Eg; - Do you mind if I take my coat off?)
- ✓ You should always hang your suit coat, even if only over the back of your chair

Wearing a Necktie- Combinations, Knots and Care

A tie is a man's way to express his personality and style.

Before you put on your tie:

- ✓ Check to make sure that the tie is clean, without any stains, grease or food spots
- ✓ Cut any loose threads on your tie. Pulling them can do damage to your tie.
- ✓ When wearing a shirt, tie and jacket, stick to a maximum of two different patterns unless you have a very solid fashion sense and know how to mix and match clothing well. Your tie should ideally be darker than the color of your shirt
- ✓ Always tie the knot in front of a mirror.
- ✓ Ensure your shirt is buttoned up, with a tie collar and have the collar up before putting the tie around your neck.
- ✓ Keep the knot of the tie tight throughout the entire tying process.
- ✓ The front of your tie should be just long enough so that the tip touches the waist of your pants.
- ✓ The general width of a tie that will not get out of style of fashion is 3.5 inches.
- ✓ Ideally, the width of a tie should match the width of the jacket's lapel. If the jacket has a wide lapel, then the tie should be wide, and if narrow, then the tie is narrow.

- ✓ So also, the knot of the tie should be proportional to the collar. It should not be so big that it spreads the collar of the shirt or forces it open, or so small that it gets lost in the collar of the shirt.

Caring for your Ties:

- ✓ A tie that is properly cared for can last forever.
- ✓ Untie your tie completely and hang up your ties. It helps take out some of the wrinkles and prevents damage.
- ✓ Knit ties can be stretched when hung, so gently roll them up and store them in a drawer.
- ✓ Ideally, ties must be hung on a rack designed for ties. Ties slip and twist on hangers and will probably fall off.
- ✓ When traveling, loosely roll ties and place them inside a pair of socks or use a tie case or box.
- ✓ Don't wear the same tie twice in a row. Ties need time to return to their normal shape

How to Tie Necktie Knots

The Four in Hand Tie Knot (Probably the simplest way to tie a neck tie)

1. Start with the wide end on your right. Extend it about 30cm (ruler length) below the narrow end of your necktie
2. Cross the wide end over the narrow, and back underneath
3. Bring the wide end around passing it across the front of the narrow
4. Pass the wide end up through the loop
5. Hold the knot loosely and pass the wide end down through the loop in front.

6. Hold the narrow end of the tie and slide the knot up snug.

The Half Windsor Knot (Medium symmetrical triangle knot

1. Start with the wide end on your right. Extend it about 30cm (ruler length) below the narrow end of your necktie.

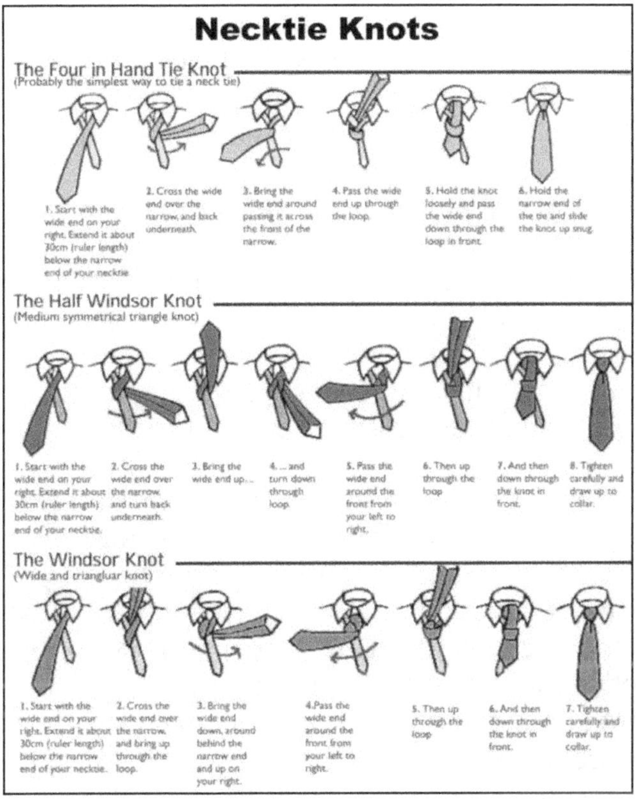

2. Cross the wide end over the narrow, and turn back underneath.
3. Bring the wide end up....
4. And turn down through loop.

5. Pass the wide end around the front from your left to right.
6. Then up through the loop
7. And then down through the knot in front
8. Tighten carefully and draw up to collar.

The Windsor Knot (Wide and triangular knot)

1. Start with the wide end on your right. Extend it about 30cm (ruler length) below the narrow end of your necktie.
2. Cross the wide end over the narrow, and bring up through the loop
3. Bring the wide end down, around behind the narrow end and up on your right
4. Pass the wide end around the front from your left to right
5. Then up through the loop
6. And then down through the knot in front.
7. Tighten carefully and draw up to collar

The meaning of colors in business that can help:

The colors you wear in professional settings and interviews can affect your mood, energy, and how others may perceive you. So you would want to wear colors that portray positive perceptions and exude confidence, sincerity, and reliability.

Here are some colors with their perceived meanings:

- ✓ Red: Action, powerful, passion and energetic
- ✓ Green: Growth, ideas, vitality and sophistication
- ✓ Blue: Inspires confidence, success and trust. Navy blue is best color for work/interviews – more likely to help create a positive vibe.
- ✓ Gold: Wealth, prosperity, luxury

- ✓ Black: Black looks classic and sophisticated, but perceived as depressing, serious or intimidating – so add a little color to black suits.
- ✓ Pink: Compassion, understanding and warmth. Pink or salmon worn by men is seen as a communicator color.
- ✓ Brown: Practical and reliable; sometimes perceived as dull
- ✓ Purple: Inventive, creative, intuitive. Dark purple can be perceived as elegant and projects authority.
- ✓ White: Clean, pure, innocent, and simple

Professional Business Attire

Men: A man's business suit is a standard item for business professional attire. Remember that your clothes should not attract more attention than the work you are doing

Ladies: Women have the versatility of choosing either a pair of dress slacks, or a skirt, with a business suit jacket. A matching pantsuit, skirt suit or even a professional dress and blazer can work. As long as your slacks are formal dress pants and look nice, they are acceptable. If you choose a skirt, it should have a comfortable fit that looks nice without being too-revealing. It's always safe to choose a skirt that hits the knee. When choosing a skirt, make sure that you can sit comfortably in public. Mini-skirts, for example, or skirts that are short and tight are inappropriate.

Informal-type pants such as jeans, sweat pants, leggings, spandex, or shorts should be avoided.

Professional Footwear: Conservative walking shoes, dress shoes, oxfords, loafers, boots, flats, dress heels, and backless shoes are acceptable for work. Not wearing stockings or socks is inappropriate.

Athletic shoes, tennis shoes, flip-flops, slippers, and any casual shoe with an open toe are not acceptable business formal footwear

Professional Accessories and Jewelry: Tasteful, professional ties, pocket squares, scarves, belts, and jewelry are encouraged. Jewelry should be worn in good taste, with limited visible body piercings

Professional Makeup and Fragrances: A professional appearance is encouraged and excessive makeup is unprofessional. Remember that some people are allergic to the chemicals in perfumes and makeup, so wear these substances with restraint

Business Casual Attire

Men: A dress shirt and tie still looks nice, for example, but a full suit isn't necessary in a business casual environment. A nice dress shirt can be worn without a tie, yet still looks professional and put together. Dress pants in a lighter color can also be another option for a casual environment. A conservative leather belt adds a nice finish to this basic business casual outfit for men.

Ladies: Tops such as button-downs, sweaters, turtle necks, and blouses, for example, are suitable for the office. A fitted suit jacket paired with a blouse is appropriate for a business casual workplace

Business Casual Footwear: Conservative athletic or walking shoes, loafers, sneakers, boots, flats, dress heels, and leather deck-type shoes are acceptable. Wearing no stockings is acceptable in warm weather. Flashy athletic shoes, flip-flops, slippers, and any shoe with open toes are not acceptable in the office.

Business Casual Accessories and Jewelry: Accessories and jewelry should be worn in good taste, with limited visible body piercings

Business Casual Makeup and Fragrances: All products should be worn in good taste. Remember that some people are allergic to the chemicals in perfumes and makeup, so wear these substances with restraint.

Casual Attire

Casual Dressing: This is for casual Fridays or casual events. In general, this means clothes that are nice, but not dressy. This look can include jeans and khaki-type pants. Jeans should be dark wash and have no holes or extreme fading. Chinos or "Dockers"- type trousers, Polo shirts (with collars), Sweater or sport jackets are fine

Grooming Checklist

What could you do to improve your image- starting right from the top of your head to the tip of your toes- your hygiene, dressing and grooming, being organized etc.

Given below is a suggested checklist to help you project the Right Image!

Physical Aspects like:

- ✓ Personal Grooming-Dress for the next level!
- ✓ Cleanliness, Breath (floss/ use mouthwash), Hair well groomed, Nails, Body Odour (light deodorant)
- ✓ Clean, Wrinkle-free and Well-Pressed/ Proper fit clothes
- ✓ Check for stains/ lint/ holes/ loose buttons
- ✓ Pleasant Colours of Clothing

- ✓ Polished shoes and in good condition (don't let heels run down)
- ✓ Socks (clean without holes, foot deodorant?)
- ✓ Clean Spectacles
- ✓ Briefcase/ handbag well polished/ in good condition
- ✓ Business Cards in pristine, crisp condition (in a holder)
- ✓ Good quality pens that write!
- ✓ Standing- shoulder square/ sitting- erect
- ✓ Good Leather Bag/ Briefcase-organized /in order/ tidy

You might like to develop your own checklist now to suit your specific country and need.
(You might like to add on to the list above)

Body Language

As we've seen, people form 90% of their opinion of us in the first 90 seconds, a good example of just how powerful first impressions are! Being dressed for success is good but not enough in the competitive times in which we live. How many people do you know that impress us with their clothes but fail to impress us in other ways? Body language is the way you stand, sit, the way you move, and the way you present yourself. A major percentage of what we communicate has nothing to do with words.
We communicate in a lot of other ways-by the way we sit, stand, tense our facial muscles, tap our fingers, shuffle our feet and uncross or cross our legs. Without saying a word, our body language is broadcasting so many things about us!
So here are some quick tips on what to do and not do!

How to Look Interested

- ✓ Make strong eye contact
- ✓ Tilt your head slightly
- ✓ Don't fidget
- ✓ Look upward
- ✓ Lean forward slightly, weight on balls of feet.

When someone is friendly, we also think of him as trustworthy, sincere and reliable.

How to Stand the Right Way

- ✓ Stand squarely in front of the person to whom you are speaking.
- ✓ It might sound strange, but you expose your heart and body.
- ✓ Don't turn sideways.
- ✓ Meet their eyes in a friendly but steady gaze.
- ✓ Smile in a warm, relaxed way
- ✓ Don't hold a book or purse in front of you or cross your arms.
- ✓ Use open hand gestures.

Maintaining the Right Physical Distance

- ✓ If you watch a crowd, you will notice that people stand at different distances from each other.
- ✓ Less than 18 inches: intimate
- ✓ 18 inches- 2.5 feet: close friends in a social gathering. You can hold out your arm and you can stick your thumb in the other person's ear! Try it!
- ✓ 2.5-4 feet: most people in a casual setting
- ✓ 4-12 feet: strangers
- ✓ 12 feet: a group of strangers
- ✓ If you get too close, the other person will grow tense or withdraw

Making Eye Contact

- ✓ The eyes have it. Well, they truly do, and can project confidence when there are no words.
- ✓ To be a good listener, let your eyes convey: "I'm listening"

Here are some Signs that can indicate Nervousness. Try to work on controlling these:

- ✓ Eyes darting back and forth
- ✓ Tensing of the body
- ✓ Contraction of the body
- ✓ Shifting one's weight from side to side
- ✓ Rocking in chair
- ✓ Crossing and uncrossing the arms or legs
- ✓ Tapping hands, fingers, or feet
- ✓ Adjusting or fiddling with pens, cups, eyeglasses, jewelry, clothing, fingernails, hair, or hands wringing hands
- ✓ Clearing the throat
- ✓ Coughing nervously
- ✓ Smiling nervously
- ✓ Biting the lip
- ✓ Looking down
- ✓ Chewing nails or picking cuticles
- ✓ Putting hands in pockets

And here are some Signs that can indicate Boredom. Try and work on controlling these too:

- ✓ Moving your body frequently
- ✓ Letting your eyes wander
- ✓ Gazing into the distance
- ✓ Glancing often at your watch
- ✓ Yawning
- ✓ Tapping fingers or feet
- ✓ Fidgeting
- ✓ Picking your fingers or nails
- ✓ Avoiding eye contact

Sitting, Standing and Walking the Right Way

The Right Way to Sit- for a Lady: If you are in someone's home or at a big social event, never sit, till you are given permission to do so. The hostess may have planned on a particular place she would like you to sit. If no one offers you, then only take the seat of your choice. Walk towards the chair with good posture. Turn and feel the chair with the back of your knees, just to make sure that no one has "accidentally" moved the chair away. Sit down, keeping your back straight and your head up, while keeping your knees together and you hands in your lap. Cross your legs at the ankle or hold your feet together. In any event, make sure your knees are together

The Right Way to Sit- for a Gentleman: Walk to the chair with good posture, and as you approach the chair, unbutton your jacket. Sit tall with your back against the chair and knees slightly apart and both feet on the floor, with your hands resting just above your knees. When you stand up, remember to re-button your jacket

Standing: When you get up, keep your feet parallel but your knees relaxed. Ensure that your spine is long and straight, with your shoulders back, stomach in, chest high, chin turned up slightly and your arms and hands relaxed.

Walking: Stand as mentioned above and step with feet slightly ahead of your body. This promotes good posture

Other Points: Never lean on anything, as it denotes a careless attitude with 99% of your "presence" being lost when you lean.

Never greet someone with a handshake across the table (the only exception of course is when you're meeting someone and both of you are seated).
Always stand up when you are shaking hands. Greeting someone from behind a desk creates an instant barrier. Instead, always greet someone as your equal

Examples of Successful Leaders Exhibiting Executive Presence

In this chapter, we will explore real-life examples of successful leaders who exhibit executive presence. These examples will illustrate how these leaders demonstrate the key characteristics of executive presence in their everyday actions and interactions.

1. **Steve Jobs**
   Steve Jobs, co-founder and former CEO of Apple Inc., is often cited as a prime example of executive presence. Jobs was known for his charismatic leadership style, visionary thinking, and ability to inspire and motivate his team. His famous keynote presentations, where he introduced groundbreaking products like the iPhone and iPad, showcased his confidence, charisma, and clear communication skills.
   Example: During one of his keynote presentations, Jobs introduced the first iPhone, captivating the audience with his enthusiasm and passion for the product. His ability to communicate the vision behind the iPhone and its revolutionary features demonstrated his executive presence and ability to influence others.
2. **Indra Nooyi**
   Indra Nooyi, former CEO of PepsiCo, is another example of a leader with strong executive presence. Nooyi was known for her strategic thinking, resilience, and ability to lead with grace and poise. She was instrumental in

reshaping PepsiCo's business strategy and expanding its product portfolio.

Example: Nooyi's leadership style was evident during the 2008 financial crisis when she steered PepsiCo through challenging economic conditions. Her calm and composed demeanor reassured investors and employees, showcasing her executive presence during a time of uncertainty.

3. **Angela Merkel**

   Angela Merkel, the former Chancellor of Germany, is renowned for her strong leadership and political acumen. Merkel's ability to lead with authority, integrity, and pragmatism has earned her respect on the global stage.

   Example: Merkel's leadership during the European migrant crisis demonstrated her executive presence. She navigated complex political challenges with empathy and decisiveness, showing her ability to lead with grace and poise in the face of adversity.

4. **Satya Nadella**

   Satya Nadella, CEO of Microsoft, is recognized for his transformative leadership style and emphasis on empathy and inclusion. Nadella's approach has revitalized Microsoft's culture and positioned the company as a leader in the tech industry.

   Example: Nadella's executive presence was evident during Microsoft's acquisition of LinkedIn. His ability to communicate the strategic rationale behind the acquisition and inspire confidence in stakeholders showcased his leadership and executive presence.

These examples highlight how successful leaders exhibit executive presence through their actions, decisions, and interactions. By studying these real-life examples, aspiring leaders can gain valuable insights into how they can develop their own executive presence and lead with confidence and impact.

Conclusion

As we conclude our journey into understanding and developing executive presence (EP), it's important to reflect on the key points and insights we've gained. Throughout this book, we've explored the definition of EP, its importance in today's world, and the various components and traits that contribute to it. We've also discussed strategies for developing and maintaining EP, along with real-life examples and stories to illustrate these concepts.

Summarizing Key Points

- ✓ Executive presence is the ability to project confidence, credibility, and authority in professional settings.
- ✓ It is essential for senior leaders as it influences how they are perceived by others and can impact their effectiveness as leaders.
- ✓ EP is not just about how you look or speak, but also about how you act and engage with others.
- ✓ The key components of EP include composure, connection, charisma, confidence, credibility, clarity, and conciseness, along with authenticity, grace, and poise.
- ✓ Developing EP requires self-awareness, continuous learning, and a willingness to step out of your comfort zone.

Encouraging Application of EP Principles in Leadership Roles

As you continue your leadership journey, I encourage you to apply the principles of executive presence in your daily interactions and decision-making. Remember that EP is not about being perfect, but about being authentic and intentional in your actions. By embodying the traits of EP, you can enhance your leadership effectiveness and inspire others to do the same.

Real-Life Example:
Sarah, a senior executive, was known for her strong executive presence. She exuded confidence and charisma in meetings, and her colleagues looked up to her as a role model. Despite facing challenges and setbacks, Sarah remained composed and focused, inspiring her team to do the same. Through her leadership, Sarah demonstrated the power of executive presence in driving success and achieving goals.

In conclusion, developing executive presence is a continuous journey that requires self-reflection, practice, and a commitment to growth. By applying the principles outlined in this book, you can enhance your EP and become a more effective and influential leader. Remember, executive presence is not just about how you present yourself; it's about how you show up in the world and the impact you have on others. Embrace your unique qualities, stay true to your values, and lead with confidence and grace.

Reflection Questions:

- ✓ What are the key takeaways from this book that you will apply to your leadership journey?
- ✓ How do you plan to integrate the principles of executive presence into your daily life and work?

- ✓ What challenges do you anticipate in developing your executive presence, and how will you overcome them?
- ✓ How will you measure your progress in enhancing your executive presence over time?
- ✓ What advice would you give to someone who is looking to improve their executive presence based on your learnings from this book?

About the Author 'GERARD ASSEY'

Gerard Assey is a Graduate in Economics, a PGD in Management (HRD) and holds a Doctorate in Leadership. Gerard holds several International Qualifications in Sales, Debt Collection, Training & Teaching, and is a 'Fellow' of the prestigious 'Institute of Sales & Marketing Management'-UK, a Certified NLP Practitioner, a 'Certified Trainer', an 'Accredited Management Teacher-Behavioral Sciences', a 'Certified Competency Facilitator', a 'Certified Management Consultant'- (the International credentials of a professional management consultant, awarded in accordance with global standards of the ICMCI); and a Certification from the University of Michigan in 'Successful Negotiation: Essential Strategies and Skills'

He is also a Member of the 'National Association of Sales Professionals' backed with several years experience in varied industries, both in India and Overseas. He also holds an 'Etiquette Consultant' Certification from the USA (by Sue Fox, Author of Best Seller: 'Business Etiquette for Dummies'. She has trained some of the top celebrities' world over). He was also a recipient of a scholarship for extensive training in Japan on 'Corporate Management for India'.

Gerard Assey is 'Founder & Chief Corporate Trainer' of the Group: '**Citius, Altius, Fortius Unlimited**'- an organization that **celebrated 20 years of Glorious Service** in 2021, focusing on 3 Core Competencies:

People. Performance. Profit; in functional areas of Sales & Marketing, HR & Organizational Development, covering Recruitment, Training & Consultancy!

Having managed organizations with large Sales Forces in India & Overseas, his specialization cover extensive areas of Sales Training (All levels - Presentation, Negotiation, Key/ Strategic Accounts Management & Managerial Skills for all sectors), Bid Proposal/ Capture Planning/ Management Trainings, Retail Sales, Customer Service & Customer Retention Programs, Training for Prevention & Collection of Debt, Self & Personal Development Programs (Time Management, Teamwork & Team Building, Business Etiquette & Personal Grooming, Leadership & Managerial Skills, People Management Skills, Train-the-Trainer etc), including preparation of Custom-designed Business Manuals for Internal (HR, Induction, and Sales etc) & External use (Instruction, User Manuals).

Gerard has successfully conducted over 6150 Trainings & Workshops (as of April '24) all across India, Middle East, Africa, Europe & S.E. Asia. Besides public programs conducted regularly, both in India & Overseas, he has some of the top names as clients whom he services from Single Owners to large Public & Government undertakings, covering all sectors, for their in-house needs.

His website: www.CollectionSkills.com is the only one in this part of the world to be featured in the 'Collections & Credit Risk Magazine-USA' under 'Who's Who in Training' and ranks TOP, along with other websites listed below on most search engines.

Gerard is author of 121 books already (April 2024)

A few of our business related books:

1. Bite-sized Bits on Commonsense Management
2. Heart to Heart on Life's Principles'
3. How to become a Successful Manager
4. The Sales Professionals' Master Workbook of S.Y.S.T.E.M.S
5. The Professional Business Email Etiquette Handbook & Guide
6. The Professional Business Video-Conferencing Etiquette Handbook & Guide
7. Professional Presentation Skills
8. Exceptional Customer Service
9. Professional Tele-Marketing Skills
10. Professional Debt Collection Skills
11. The G.R.E.A.T. Sales & Service Workbook
12. Sales Training Advantage for Results (*The Ultimate Sales Training Manual to enable you stand out as a S.T.A.R.*)
13. CEO Daily Planner & Organizer
14. The Sales Professionals' Master Daily Planner
15. The Professional Debt Collector's Master Daily Planner
16. My Daily Planner & Organizer
17. MY EMERGENCY INFORMATION RECORD (Family Emergency & Peace of Mind Planner)
18. The Ultimate Therapist & Counselors Planner and Organizer
19. Building an Ethical Workplace
20. Managing Relationships at Work
21. Managing Business Meetings Effectively
22. Effective Delegation Skills
23. Goal Setting for Success
24. B2B Selling by Email
25. Professional Business Etiquette & Grooming
26. Dining Etiquette & Table Manners
27. Effective Networking Skills
28. Grooming, Etiquette & Manners for Teens, Young Adults & Future Leaders
29. Inter-Personal Skills
30. Get Ready, Get Hired!
31. Selling in a Recession
32. Effective Receivables Management in an Economic Downturn!
33. Real Estate & Property Sales Training

34. Credit Sales & Accounts Receivable Management
35. Selling Skills for Real Estate & Property Advisors
36. Take G.R.E.A.T. C.A.R.E!
37. Spa, Salon & Health Club Selling Skills
38. Selling Travel, Holiday & MICE Services
39. Selling Skills for Spa's, Salons & Health Clubs
40. Retailing in Salons & Spas
41. Selling Holiday, Vacation, Tours & Packages
42. The Power of Sales Referrals
43. Selling Luxury
44. Technical Selling Skills
45. Financial Advisors Sales Training
46. Dealing with Burnout at Work Monopolize Your Markets
47. Selling to Affluent Customers
48. Growing up with Grace
49. Financial Selling Skills
50. *The Effective Manager's Guide: Key Skills to Thrive*
51. From Aspiring to Inspiring: A Guide for New Managers on the Rise
52. The Power of Focus
53. Selling with Integrity: Sell Like Jesus The Perfect Role Model!
54. 31 Habits of Champions: Your 31-Day Journey to Greatness
55. Rejecting Grasshopper Talk: From Grasshopper to Giant-Killer-*Defeating Giants Daily!*
56. Navigate the AI-Powered Future of Bid & Proposals: Up-Skill to Stay Relevant with Alternative Career Paths & Opportunities
57. Hiring Sales Winners
58. Present with Impact
59. Success Unlocked: *Breaking Free from Habits that Hold You Back*
60. Complaints to Cheers, Feedback to Gold: Mastering Complaints Management
61. Thriving Together: *Cultivating Diversity, Equity, and Inclusion*
62. Coaching Skills for Sales Managers
63. Soaring to Success in Business & Leadership: Swifter, Higher, Stronger!
64. From Classroom to Podium: A Student's Guide to Powerful Public Speaking & Presentation Skills

65. Developing Self-Discipline
66. The CEO's 31-Day Power Plan: Unlocking Success through Essential Traits
67. Credibility Matters
68. A Winning Attitude
69. Bid & Proposal Management Using AI
70. Sales Forecasting: A Practical & Proven Guide to Strategic Sales Forecasting
71. Elevate & Energize: *50 Dynamic & Fun Activities for Peak Workplace Morale*
72. 'Sales SOS! Sales on Fire! *30 Days to Conquer Chaos & the Nightmares of Success!'*
73. Mastering Sales Managerial Skills: *Building High-Performing Teams & Driving Exceptional Results*
74. Eagle-Eyed Leadership: Unleashing the Power of 31 Lessons from Eagles
75. The Ultimate Employee Training Guide: *Training Today, Leading Tomorrow*
76. Being More Accountable at Work
77. Creating a Culture of Continuous Improvement
78. Effective Questioning & Listening Skills
79. The Power of Value Selling
80. The Growth Mindset
81. Mastering Professional Help Desk Skills
82. The Power to Lead with Empathy
83. Being Prepared: The Key to Unlocking Success
84. Youthful Spark-Youth Energizers, Activities and Games-Igniting the Fun in Youth
85. Ignite your Motivation for Success
86. Elevate Your Executive Presence: *Your Roadmap to Executive Excellence*

Besides regularly contributing to business & trade journals, including international ones such as the 'Creative Training Techniques' and the 'Sales News' of the U.S.A, He is also a member of several prestigious bodies & trade associations, having participated in many Conferences & Workshops in India & Overseas.

Prior to his last assignment of leading & managing a large MNC as head, Gerard had a 3-year stint in the Middle East as a Consultant with a leading British Consultancy Firm.

As the past 'Official Country Representative' for the International Business Award- 'THE STEVIES'-(the business world's own Oscar) for about 4 years- he ensured a few Indian companies that qualify for the same every year!

Gerard can be contacted at:
Email: training@Sales-Training.in,training@CollectionSkills.com
Websites:

www.Sales-Training.in
www.EtiquetteWorks.in
www.CollectionSkills.com
www.RetailSalesTraining.in
www.SalesTrainingIndia.com
www.ManualPreparation.com
www.TrainingWithPuppets.com
www.FirstContactAcademy.com
www.SalesAndMarketingRecruiter.com

Our TRAININGS that can help your team

- ✓ **Sales Effectiveness**: Selling Skills for any Sector: Service/ Logistics/ FMCG Realty/ Insurance & Finance/ Media/ SPA's, Health Clubs & Salons/ Key Account Management, Effective Negotiation Skills/ Bid & Proposal Management Skills/ Retail Sales Training: Any Sector (Auto, Jewelry, Clothing, Luxury etc)
- ✓ **Customer Service Skills**-Complaints Handling & Customer Retention
- ✓ **Debt Prevention & Collection Skills**
- ✓ **Etiquette & Grooming**
- ✓ **Leadership & Managerial Skills**
- ✓ **Self & Personal Development Skills**: Presentation Skills/ Effective Communication Skills/Business Proposal Writing Skills/ Problem Solving & Decision Making Skills/ Empowering Secretaries-The perfect PA! (For Secretaries & PA's)/ Effective Time Management/ Teamwork & Teambuilding/ P.R.I.D.E- **P**ersonal **R**esponsibility **I**n **D**elivering **E**xcellence

www.ingramcontent.com/pod-product-compliance
Lightning Source LLC
Chambersburg PA
CBHW062109160726
48282CB00026B/730
* 9 7 8 8 1 9 7 1 1 2 1 1 9 *